Making Sense of Section 17

A study for the Department of Health

Implementing Services for Children In Need, Within the 1989 Children Act.

Co-Directors

Jane Aldgate,
University of Leicester
Jane Tunstill,
University of Keele

Published for Department of Health under licence from the Controller of Her Majesty's Stationery Office.

ISBN 011 321914 8

Second Impression 2003

Complementary titles also available from TSO include:

The Children Act Volume 1	Court Orders	ISBN 0 11 321371 9
The Children Act Volume 2	Family Support, Day Care and Educational Provision for Young Children	ISBN 0 11 321372 7
The Children Act Volume 3	Family Placements	ISBN 0 11 321375 1
The Children Act Volume 4	Residential Care	ISBN 0 11 321430 8
The Children Act Volume 5	Independent Schools	ISBN 0 11 321373 5
The Children Act Volume 6	Children with Disabilities	ISBN 0 11 321452 9
The Children Act Volume 7	Guardians Ad Litem and other Court Related Issues	ISBN 0 11 321471 5
The Children Act Volume 8	Private Fostering and Miscellaneous	ISBN 0 11 321473 1
The Children Act Volume 9	Adoption Issues	ISBN 0 11 321474 X
The Children Act Volume 10	Index	ISBN 0 11 321538 X
The Challenge of Partnership in Child Protection: Practice Guide published January 1995		ISBN 0 11 321825 7

Acknowledgements

We would like to record our gratitude for the hardwork and commitment of Graham McBeath and Rita Ozolins, our research associates, who worked with us on the study, and we wish them well in their new jobs.

We are extremely grateful for the help and support way beyond the call of funding from our colleagues in the Department of Health, especially Dr. Carolyn Davies, Jane Scott and Angela Williams from the Research and Development Division, Rupert Hughes CBE and Valerie Brasse, from the Community Services Division, Wendy Rose and her colleagues in the Social Services Inspectorate, Peter Smith, Alan Jones and Richard Balfe and Jim Stokoe, whose statistical advice was invaluable. We are indebted to colleagues in universities for their support: at the University of Oxford, Professor Stein Ringen, Teresa Smith, Michael Noble, Marie Bradley, David Hawley, Janet Hendron, Susan Dyson, Clive Payne and Martin Range; at the University of East Anglia, Professor June Thoburn and Jane Gibbons; at the Dartington Social Research Unit, Professor Spencer Millham, Dr. Roger Bullock and Dr. Micheal Little; at the University of Leicester, Pauline Hardiker, Dr. J. Owusu-Bempah, Lynn Smolinski and Malayne Bowler. We could not have done this study without the advice, encouragement and participation of senior colleagues in Social Services Departments: Janey Held, Margaret Goldie, Richard Heyes, Jane Streather, Ian White, Mike Simm, Paul Sutton, Ann Jamieson, Louise Bessant, Brian Waller. We would also like to thank members of the Audit Commission, especially Clair Backman, Dr. Ross Tristem, Beverly Fitzsimons and Colin Bott, with whom we had a robust exchange of views at a crucial stage in the study. Lastly, we must express our gratitude to all local authority officers who persevered with and returned to us the complex and challenging questionnaire upon which the quantitative data was based.

Jane Aldgate
Jane Tunstill

October 1995

Contents

Chapter 1

Introduction and Background to Study

> There are unique advantages for children in experiencing normal family life in their own birth family and every effort should be made to preserve the child's home and family links. A wide variety of services, including short-term out of home placement, may need to be employed in order to sustain some families through particularly difficult periods. The provision of services to help maintain the family home is a requirement of the Children Act 1989.
>
> *(Principles and Practice in Guidance and Regulations, Department of Health, 1989, Chapter 2, para. 5).*

The Children Act is based on a clear set of principles which were made explicit in the White Paper which preceded the Act and were developed at length in the complementary volume Principles and Practice in Guidance and Regulations. Drawing in particular on 'parental responsibility' and 'non-intervention in family life unless necessary' (Family and Child Care Law Training Group 1989), a fundamental message can be identified, namely, that children in families matter. The stability of family life is of paramount importance for the happiness and welfare of children. Their life-chances and opportunities for effective citizenship are importantly influenced by upbringing and life-experience. Central to this developmental process are both the range and effectiveness of supports available to children in their families. When intra-familial supports to the child fail or are absent to the detriment of that child, the state has a duty to offer aid to the family, or directly to the child to promote his or her welfare. However the state then has a duty to withdraw when parents are once more able to discharge their responsibilities to their children; the state is not there to act as a 'controlling guardian', but rather to provide support services to children in need and their families as and when required. It should be accepted that it is *normal* for families to need support from professionals from time to time. Consequently, services on offer should be responsive to the normal vicissitudes of family life. Such services must take account of differences of race, culture, language and religion.

It is helpful to provide a policy context for the translation of these principles into law in the Children Act 1989.

The evolution of 'in need'

Section 17 of the Children Act 1989 is theoretically complex. It could be argued that investigating implementation of policy and practice requires a correspondingly broad conceptual framework. In addition to the professional and organisational challenges in respect of implementation, Section 17 represents a three-dimensional change from earlier legislation.

Firstly, there is a departure from a broad assumption of practice based on **social work advice and counselling** to a wider remit of **service delivery**; secondly, from a relatively narrow concept of **prevention** of reception into care to the broader concept of **family support** and **promotion of welfare** and thirdly, from a concern about an **undifferentiated group** of children to a specific group who are defined as **children in need**.

The Changes in the law

The Children Act has marked a radical change in approach to family support which has been summarised by Rose (1992):

> The Children Act places a general duty on local authorities to safeguard and promote the welfare of children in their area who are in need and, subject to that duty, to promote the upbringing of such children by their families. The new emphasis in Section 17 is for local authorities to work with the family and child in the family home and for local authorities to work with or facilitate the work of others.
>
> This is reinforced in Section 27, with the new duty on other agencies to assist local authorities in the performance of their duties. This is a vital opportunity for local authorities to influence others in the way they work with families (partnership in all aspects) and to encourage multi-disciplinary working and mutual understanding between all agencies.
>
> The new provisions of the Children Act enable a range of services such as accommodation not to be seen as a breakdown in preventive service but as a positive measure of family support. They allow for the development of imaginative and flexible services in partnership and in support of families with users' views fully taken into account and services assessed against the welfare check list of Section 1. Such developments have a relatively recent history.
>
> *(Rose 1992, pp. ix-x).*

Section 17 embraces these intended changes identified by defining a child in need widely.

Section 17(10) states that a child is 'in need' if:

(a) he is unlikely to achieve or maintain, or to have the opportunity of achieving or maintaining, a reasonable standard of health or development without the provision for him of services by a local authority;

(b) his health or development is likely to be significantly impaired, or further impaired, without the provision for him of such services; or

(c) he is disabled.

Additionally, the Guidance and Regulations Vol. 2 states:

> The definition of need . . . is deliberately wide to reinforce the emphasis on preventive support and services to families. It has three categories: a reasonable standard of health or development; significant impairment of health or development; significant impairment of health or development and disablement. It would not be acceptable for an authority to exclude any of these three - for example, by confining services to children at risk of significant harm which attracts the duty to investigate under Section 47
>
> *(Department of Health 1991b, para. 2.4).*

Thus, family support must have a broad base and not be restricted to services for those already identified as being in serious difficulties. Local authorities have to identify the extent of need in their area and make decisions about the priorities for service provision based on that identification. As Gibbons suggests, family support provisions therefore 'have an important part to play in "buffering" the effects of stress on vulnerable families.' (Gibbons 1992, p. 3).

As Rose (1992) has suggested, there may be many barriers to the development of family support services, such as the prioritising of child abuse and referrals, financial and political considerations, measuring the effectiveness of services, developing coherent strategies, policies and services that are flexible and accounting for the short term perspective of social services and funding in the voluntary sector.

Family support in an historical context

In monitoring the extent to which local authorities have attempted to, or have achieved the intentions of Section 17, account must be taken of two of the least resolved concepts in social policy or social work literature which have provoked much debate: prevention and family support.

(i) Prevention

Child care law and policy is often depicted as a perennial pendulum swing between notions characterised crudely as **prevention** and **protection** (Macleod

1982, McGowan and Meezan 1983, Fox Harding 1991, Holman 1988), with general agreement that 1948 marks the beginning of the current debate (Heywood 1965, Watson 1973, Packman 1975). As Fox Harding (1991) and George and Wilding (1985) stress, account must be taken of the influence of ideology on both the selection of goals for child care practice and the priority given to research exercises through which to measure their outcome. However, across a range of studies deriving from several value perspectives, two dominant strands can be identified in the literature on prevention:

(a) **attempts at definition, including the clarification of those outcomes to be prevented** (Parker 1980, Jordan 1987, Holman 1988, Hardiker et al 1991, Gardner 1992, Gibbons 1992).

Although Fuller (1987) has questioned the value of schematic approaches to the problem of definition, a common theme in many of these discussions is the invocation of the health terminology of primary, secondary and tertiary prevention. While most social work activity is seen as deriving from secondary and tertiary objectives, writers differ in the extent to which they apply notions of primary prevention. At one extreme, Holman (1988, pp. 119-124) for example talks of 'preventing children enduring social disadvantage within their families', while the Seebohm Report (1968, para. 429) includes the 'prevention of social distress'. Billis (1984) on the other hand is sceptical about the ability of social work to address issues such as homelessness and low income. Hardiker et al. (1991, pp. 40-41) add 'quaternary' prevention to the list, to mean the early restoration of children who have been placed away from home.

(b) **accounts of attempts to monitor or evaluate specific projects** (Thoburn 1980, Jones 1985, Gibbons et al. 1990; Farmer and Parker 1991, Fuller 1992)

These may initially appear to provide a more conclusive way forward, but the distinction between this approach and attempts at definition is on closer examination blurred, in that evaluative studies presume a clarity about what is to be prevented.

'A comprehensive social work model of preventive services did achieve positive, albeit modest, results in preventing and delaying foster care among poor, minority, female headed multi-problem families in New York City in the mid-1970s' (Jones 1985, p. 153).

To some extent, such studies are a product of the policy era in which they are undertaken and, it could be argued, have a necessarily circular relationship with policy and legislation. In line with the 1969 and 1980 Acts therefore, the dominant focus of studies before 1968 was on the prevention of reception into care or of juvenile delinquency, though one bonus of a relatively narrow legislative focus is its implications for the selection of indicators such as rates of admission to accommodation or care.

However, Fuller suggests this can give a misleading tidy picture:

> The most straightforward preventive category, preventing entry to care, did figure in the analysis, but not significantly more often than other kinds of objective, and the Project was really engaged in a broader and less easily definable range of tasks than its stated aims.
>
> *(Fuller 1992, p. 100).*

This study of a voluntary provided project echoes Packman et al. (1986) in questioning whether the task of social work or the aim of research evaluation should be limited to a concern with prevention.

(ii) Family Support

The concept of Family Support as a successor to prevention of admission to accommodation or care has its roots in a range of research studies, including Packman's finding that parents received no other service if they did not get an offer of care for their children. It also acknowledges that, as indicated by Fuller (1992), Hardiker et al. (1989) and Farmer and Parker (1991) amongst others, the offering of resources to the child in the community within the family, not only after removal is a central part of preventive social work.

Research findings however, provide no conclusive indication of the operational limits of **family support** as opposed to **prevention**. Gibbons (1990) is an exception in explicitly linking the two terms in her investigation. She described the effects which different levels of voluntary family and child provision have on the support available to families and concluded that broad-based family support can be achieved through independent family and child care projects, (though there was no evidence that social workers in the project area altered their practice to make use of the projects).

The investigation of family support has more often taken one or two forms: studies of individual family support organisations, (Cox et al. 1992, Stalker 1990) or probably more frequently, overview studies of types of provision, such as family centres or day-care (Van der Eyken 1984, Smith 1992, Cannan 1993 Orlik et al. 1991).

The distinction between prevention and family support remains to be finalised, but it could be argued that in terms of access to, and the nature of the services accessed, family support implies a more influential or autonomous role for users. There may also be differences in the extent of targeting users of services. Prevention denotes an awareness of potential risk, and therefore a more targeted population of service recipients, while family support is more diffuse, both in intention, and is therefore less amenable to targeting (Tunstill 1992).

The concept of 'in need'

The concept of children in need in the 1989 Act represents a fusing of the concepts of prevention and family support; ' .. the Act takes a quantum leap from the old restricted notions of "prevention" to a more positive outreaching duty of "support for children and families" ' (Packman and Jordan 1991, p.323). It combines in one legal category, children at some greater level as well as lesser risk to their health or welfare (Section 17 (1)). It draws on ideas about prevention and family support in conjunction with an apparent confidence that 'need' can be agreed, assessed and measured (Section 17(10)).

The new definition of in need also acknowledges the essential social work role in protecting children from significant harm. As Shaw et al. have pointed out:

> There is no necessary conflict between the principles of family support and of child protection provided that everyone concerned in implementing the Act keeps in mind the paramount importance of the children's welfare and safety as the basic need (Shaw, et al. 1991, p. 20)

However, little previous research evidence exists of an operational consensus on this topic; more often than not, a picture emerges of the child as a 'bundle of needs with adult caretakers or state agencies disputing the definition of such needs and the ability to provide them' (King and Piper 1990, pp. 61-66).

The current research project attempts to explore how far Children Act implementation of Section 17 in English local authorities has succeeded in overcoming historical constraints on the development of family support and moving towards achieving the complex aims and objectives of the Act.

The purpose of the study is to present a broad national picture of the range of approaches to implementing Section 17 adopted by the majority of English social services departments and their local authorities during the first eighteen months implementation. The study provides an essential context for identifying, exploring and understanding issues which have arisen in the course of early implementation. A further aim of the study has been to inform the development of appropriate instruments for the revised statistical returns from social services departments on Section 17. An interim report on the study findings was submitted to the Department of Health in November 1992. Early findings were included in Chapter 3 of *Children Act 1989, A Report by the Secretaries of State for Health and for Wales on the Children Act 1989 in pursuance of their duties under Section 83(6) of the Act. Cm 2144 HMSO, 1992*

The Study had two stages:

- The initial stage of the project was based on a postal questionnaire to all local authorities in England sent out in Autumn 1992 to enquire into their implementation of Section 17; and on policy documents relating to the implementation of Section 17.
- This was followed up by semi-structured interviews with a case study sample of 10 senior managers and team leaders in 10 authorities focused on the implementation process. This enables the essentially quantitative questionnaire responses to be amplified by qualitative data (see also Methodology, Appendix I, pages 59-66).

The study investigated four areas which are explored in the next four chapters:

- *Chapter 2* looks at the steps taken by local authorities to ascertain the extent of need in their areas, including the use of predetermined groups and other data. It also outlines the problems involved with data collection and definition of statutory duties.
- *Chapter 3* describes the experience of working across the organisational divide: how much local authorities have been able to build on previous good relationships with other agencies both within and outside the local authority. It examines the patterns of consultation and circulation of material adopted by local authorities to the implementation process.
- *Chapter 4* explores how local authorities have decided upon priorities for service delivery and how they perceive their varying responsibilities for family support.
- *Chapter 5* describes the patterns of service delivery for Section 17 and outlines the progress made towards service provision based on a mixed economy of welfare.
- *Chapter 6* summarises the findings and their implications for the development of policy and practice.

Chapter 2

Identifying the Key Challenges for Implementation

> For many the processes of implementing the Children Act began at the preparatory stages as soon as the Bill received Royal Assent way back in November 1989 and indeed for a minority of colleagues implementation was seen as a process which commenced on the date that the Act itself came into force last October. Others will say that implementation has more subtle meanings and is an ongoing process.
>
> (SSI 1992, p. 1 of Executive summary)

The earlier London SSI study quoted above (in which one of the two authors participated) was the first substantial monitoring exercise in response to the Children Act implementation. Its conclusions reflect the findings of the current study: that implementation varied among the local authorities surveyed in respect of timing duration and the personnel involved.

Implementing the Children Act in general and Section 17 in particular involved local authorities in several key stages. These did not necessarily occur in the same order. The constraints of a national study meant that, while research was able to produce information about the dominant activities within each of the stages, it could not produce reliable information about the sequence within which all 82 local authorities participating in the study had undertaken the respective tasks involved. Interviews with senior personnel from 10 authorities indicated that it would be a mistake to assume a common procedural logic to the process of implementation. It was clear that individual local characteristics and circumstances inevitably caused a good deal of variation. In addition, there were differences in the process of implementation. There was evidence, for example, that some local authorities undertook more than one task simultaneously. Others proceeded step by step. The interviews provided examples of the various ways in which some local authorities tackled each of the tasks of implementation. It was also possible to show that, although there were different patterns in the process of implementation, and authorities were at different stages of developing their policies and practice, there was a good deal of common ground in relation to the tasks undertaken in the early stages of implementation.

The main identifiable tasks for implementing Section 17 of the Children Act were:

- setting up implementation groups;
- collecting data on which to make decisions;
- ascertaining the extent of need;
- consulting other agencies about policy documents;
- writing and disseminating policy documents;
- consulting with other organisations on the basis of the documents distributed;
- identifying groups of children for priority access to services.

In some cases some stages were mutually exclusive; in others, all stages were undertaken.

Organising implementation

1 Setting up implementation groups

From the interviews with senior managers, it seems that Children Act implementation began in many social services departments with the setting up of an implementation group composed of senior managers, policy officers, often an Assistant Director of Social Services and, sometimes, elected members. Though some authorities deferred the process of Children Act implementation until they had drafted their Community Care Plans (there was evidence from the policy documents that one authority postponed work on the Act until early 1991), most began planning early in 1990. Once the basic planning was done, two or three officers would prepare firstly, a report for the Social Services Committee, and secondly, a more general report for elected members as a whole.

Much of the basic work was undertaken without reference to agencies other than social services or to users. So at the early stages, it seems that consultation was somewhat limited. Some authorities, however, did engage in a more elaborate exercise whereby, subsequent to the initial deliberations of the implementation group, as many as 12 sub-groups of middle ranking officers led by a principal or senior practitioner would explore implementation strategies for various parts of the Act. In some cases they would undertake consultation work with other agencies inside and outside of the local authority.

The role of elected members varied. Our interviews suggest that sometimes the expectation was that members would endorse the social services department's recommendations on the stance the authority might take in regard to Section 17 implementation without too much prior debate. But there was evidence that, in some authorities, the participation of elected members was ensured early on. In one county, members were given an introduction to the Act by late 1989 and provided with financial estimates of costs and indications of how the social services department would like to respond to the provisions of the Act. Their implementation process can be summarised thus:

1 Decision on handling of implementation by senior management

2 Development section set up consisting of 3 children and families managers who would inform members about the Act and the county's possible response.

3 Setting up of 8 groups to give consideration to the implementation of various sections of the Act – children in need group, accommodation group . . . and so forth.

4 Focus on training and induction. This authority then linked up with another county social services department to provide a video training package (which was then sold on to other social services departments).

Co-ordination between groups was managed by senior officers, and members were kept informed of the implementation process at all stages by this group.

Implementation can be seen both as an initial phase and an ongoing process so it was of interest to ascertain whether members of the implementation group had stayed together to oversee the development of implementation. Senior managers suggested that, by and large, by the time of the study interviews, the implementation groups had been dispersed, but in most cases, the personnel involved had remained in children and families work with usually at least one former implementation group member remaining as a Children's Act officer or in some similar post. Where a senior manager at the level of assistant director headed the group, it was quite possible that they would continue to co-ordinate Children Act development on a less formal basis. Only in one authority had all members of the implementation group left Children Act related work. In fact all but one had left the authority!

2 Agreeing the intentions of the Act

There was considerable variance in how social services initially perceived the Act but within this two main approaches dominated:–

(a) seeing the Act as an opportunity to develop child care policy within the new philosophy of the Act;

(b) seeing the Act primarily as a reformulation of existing duties with the additional implementation of some new duties.

As an example of the first type of response, one officer observed that:

> Our links with Children Act researchers and the results of their study meant that this authority had a good grasp of the principles of the Act from the earliest days. We felt then, and we still do . . . that this authority's interpretation and understanding of the Act would be in agreement with the intentions of the Department of Health . . . It was important to get over [to staff] the philosophy of the Act, and not to just inform them of their duties and how to execute them within the terms of our authority's policy.

It was clear that some local authorities were confident about implementation of the Act and felt it important to communicate to social workers and other personnel the idea that it entailed not just a response to specific duties and requests for services but that there was a need to embrace new principles and translate these into practice.

The second type of response seemed to be more concerned with particular duties and aspects of the new legislation. In a southern authority, for example, the officer interviewed said:

> Much consideration of the Act had been led by its financial and budgeting implications, but . . . there are specific issues which are important such as working with young people, day care registration, and the need for developing voluntary partnerships with parents . . . but we take a positive approach to the unity of the Act.

One authority facing financial difficulties and problems in recruiting staff focused on the need to address these issues within the implementation. Consequently, they adopted an attitude of concentrating on the necessary rather than the desirable:

> The Act expresses a greater concern about child protection, so we need more field work posts . . . we've had to come to terms with our overspending worries, and we have had to make some redirections of staff into our children and families teams . . . but we are particularly concerned to develop our services for children looked after and those leaving care.

Others were equally cautious, seeing the Act as having considerable implications for the organisational and financial aspects of social services. A few saw the Act as yet a further burden on top of the Community Care Act and as problematic in resource terms:

> We felt at the time that some workers would see the Act as renegotiating the terms of existing legislation, and it would be difficult to encourage them to see the Act as a whole.

3 Developing policy statements

One early major task for those implementing the Act was to design policy in line with the requirements for local authorities to:

> develop effective strategies and policies and provide practitioners with a robust framework with which to work. (Guidance and Regulations, Department of Health, 1991, vol. 2, para 1.1)

The starting point for developing policies varied between authorities. It was clear that some started planning as early as 1989. Although there was a long 'run-in period', some policy statements were being designed only shortly before the legislation came into force.

Reasons for the variation in Children Act planning timescales in various authorities included the need to digest fully the Act in its final form, the pressure to prepare for the Community Care Act; ongoing work with the Criminal Justice Act; local authority budgeting problems; and in a few cases, co-operation with elected members. It was clear that social services departments took the lead in developing policy statements. From a review of policy documents available between July and October 1991, it seemed that often neither personnel in different departments of the local authorities, nor elected members, had enough time for careful consideration of these documents between publication and 14th October 1991. This however was different from the more elaborate consultation process which was evident later in relation to service provision (see Chapter 3).

Interviews indicated that consultation in relation to developing policy documents with elected members was often done on an ad hoc basis in relation to specific issues. Members were sometimes only consulted about the 'prioritisation-of-needs' structure in relation to likely patterns of service provision and on budgeting and costings rather than being involved in the evolution of the general principles underpinning policy statements. One authority, in a three page document of **children in need**, merely set out the Section 17 definition of need, the requirement in Regulations and Guidance to make decisions on the priorities for services provision in their area, and a three level model of priority categories. The document concluded by indicating that, in the main, priorities would consist of child protection work and children accommodated or at risk of criminal proceedings. On this basis elected members were 'requested to agree the proposed approach to service provision for children in need and their families'. Users, it was noted, were to be consulted later in the process. In this case, financial aspects were not discussed. This document was circulated to the Social Services Committee on the 12th September, 1991, one month before implementation. In another case, members, mostly new to the work of the social services committee, could contribute little to the Children Act implementation and so social services officers had effectively a free hand to design policies.

There were minority exceptions as the following extracts from one policy statement shows:

> In general, the following categories of children will be regarded as **in need** within the definition of the Children Act in this authority.
>
> 1 Children with disabilities
>
> 2 Children at risk of abuse or neglect.
>
> 3 Children who are delinquent or at risk of becoming delinquent.
>
> 4 Children separated form their parents by reason of divorce, hospitalisation, parent in prison, immigration restrictions, and so on.
>
> 5 Children with caring responsibilities (eg teenage parents, children of disabled parents).
>
> 6 Children whose home conditions are unsatisfactory, eg those who are homeless, in temporary or substandard accommodation or accommodation for homeless families.
>
> 7 Children who may be broadly defined as living in poverty and at high risk of family breakdown - eg children whose parents are on low wages or income support, in one-parent families, overcrowded conditions, large families with limited support etc.

Ascertaining the extent of need

It is clear from our findings that most local authorities approached the problems of ascertaining the extent of need with some trepidation. The Act states:

> Every local authority shall take reasonable steps to identify the extent to which there are children in need within their area.
>
> (Schedule 2 Pt. I, 1(1))

While the general requirement to ascertain the extent of need is clear, it could be argued that the steps by which this task should be undertaken are open to different interpretation. There are, for example, major differences in an approach based essentially on the calculation of a sum total of need individually assessed (through individual referrals) and one based on predetermined groups of children in need identified through the collection of extensive data e.g. geographic and demographic information and data from several agencies. From the interviews, it seemed that policy documents which could have been based on extensive data collection were often developed before the data had been collected.

The more sophisticated documents recognised the importance of a local definition but it was disappointing that, for may social services departments, discussion of what the definition of 'in need' meant was not related to local policies. A scrutiny of the documents revealed that, in some cases, they contained no more than simple replications of the wording of in need in the Children Act to which were attached a list of priority categories for service delivery and or provision.

How need was ascertained

Table 1 (page 67) indicates that local authorities used a variety of individual and combined ways of ascertaining the total population of children in need in their area. These included referrals; membership of a predetermined group; a combination of referral and predetermined group membership; other means, including using demographic information. There was little difference either regionally or between different types of authority in the spread of information used.

It can be seen from the table that the most popular method of ascertaining need was by a combination of **referral** and **predetermined group membership** adopted by 37 (45%) of local authorities. **Referrals only** accounted for 22 (27%). This contrasts dramatically with using **membership of a predetermined group** only 4 (5%) of local authorities.

It is perhaps not surprising that there was a mix of approaches. The concept of referral is a relatively straightforward one, common to previous child care legislation and the 1989 Act. 'Predetermined group' is a new and potentially rather more complex concept.

Sources of data to ascertain need

While referrals can be counted in a traditional way, it is more difficult to understand how local authorities estimated the proportions of children in their area who would accord with the headings of the predetermined groups. There is a presumption in the legislation that local authorities would have access to data which would enable them to identify their local predetermined groups of children as well as produce totals of children referred.

The study explored the sources of data used to ascertain the extent of need whether it was by referral, predetermined groups or a combination of both and, as a result, a picture emerged of the data collection practices across local authorities.

The position had changed slightly from the interim report: various and combined data sources were used more frequently than at first thought. Around a quarter of social services (19) said they were using 'in house' data, meaning within the social services department but the predominant approach was a combination of 'in house' and other local agencies, 52 (63%). A minority used the data from the Audit Commission, 12 (15%) and OPCS 4 (5%), academic institutions 5 (6%). There were also other minority combinations of local and national data (Table not shown).

Local authorities used data to focus upon population numbers, disabled children, numbers of children looked after, ethnicity, numbers in temporary accommodation, details about under eights and those children in trouble with the police, drawing a distinction between numbers cautioned and numbers prosecuted. Authorities were asked to self-report their uses of data, so it may be there are some accidental omissions but it is of interest that information on educational matters such as exclusions and truanting was rarely mentioned.

Problems in collecting data

The collection of data was clearly not always straightforward as senior managers confirmed in interview.

The political dimension

There was a political dimension which may have influenced the course of events. In one case the efforts put into data collection changed markedly with a change of administration:

> The extent of need was a political issue for our authority, members [who were very involved in Children Act implementation] of the ruling group discouraged us from finding out the extent of need . . . but the change in political control led to a positive encouragement in doing this work.

It should be said that the raison d'être for this was the suspicion that the more extensive the extent of need identified, the greater the financial commitments that might have to be made.

Problems of de-centralisation

Where there was a decentralised approach to data collection - data collection being done by teams in each area of county, for instance, there was a problem of consistency of data returned to County Hall. One interviewee noted that:

> We are split into 31 localities, each locality collects the kind of data they think they need . . . so it means that across the county there is a multiplicity of methods for data collection. Broadly collection is led by the groups we have identified as priority groups, but types of data

> collected varies. We do however, have a small planning and performance and review team which tries to collate and monitor the returns from the localities.

It seemed therefore from both interviews and our postal questionnaire that the process of data collection for children in need in any one area was often not systematic; instead it was dependent on whether a team had collated figures or not; whether local audits had been done in recent years by the social services department or an outside agency and so forth. The data collected was often scattered, of varying sample size, and unconnected such that it could not serve to provide a comprehensive picture of children in need in a local authority. It is possible to draw a distinction between collecting data and collating data. Most authorities seem to be doing the first, but not the second. In their policy documents, many local authorities noted the importance of data collection. The shortcomings of their activity probably say more about the lack of social services research staff and technical problems than about any lack of commitment on the part of the local authority in the execution of its duties.

The Community Care Act and Children's Services Plans

For some authorities the undertaking of research for the Community Care Act had given a lead to data collection for the Children Act. It appears that many social services departments are using a common pre-coded form for referrals. Several of the authorities interviewed stated that they had used the same data collection structure for both Acts and, in some cases, the same priority categories. Only one authority responded in the questionnaire that there was no relation between the two types of data collection; in interview, however it was suggested that this was largely because this authority had undertaken very little data collection at all- in part due to software failures.

All those managers interviewed felt that the preparation of the Children's Services Plans was far from advanced (this was during the summer of 1993). One team leader candidly said:

> At present we have no service plan . . . there has been a specific decision taken [by members] to take it slowly . . . no-one is to do it. We will of course eventually move toward drawing it up.

In decentralised arrangements, there were mixed views on the impact of this type of structure on data gathering. For some, plans were likely to be a problem as different localities had gathered data on different groups of children. As one officer from just such an authority put it:

> Because of this [decentralisation] we're in a bit of a muddle . . . but we're doing it though..

But this is not necessarily the case with all decentralised authorities. Another officer reported:

> Decentralisation helps this process [data gathering] . . . as we can focus in on problems specific to localities and go into some detail. What we do is to agree data priorities with local managers ensuring that a core set of data is collected as well as data on local conditions. Local managers have a specific budget to do this work. Given this, we feel that the data for the Children's Services Plans inadequately reflects what a local authority is doing in response to needs.

Technical problems of recording need

Another problem which hampered the gathering of adequate data upon which to ascertain need arose from the variations in research proficiency and hardware between local authorities. Some respondents alluded to serious deficits in hardware and software.

> This was a headache – we had so many computer problems.

> Our SOSCIS system is not yet fully operational, we are sorting this out with the software company.

> We rely on computers . . . we don't really have enough of them yet . . .

There seemed to be several reasons for these technical problems:

- lack of appropriate software packages;
- variability in scale and scope of research units;
- inadequate staffing for data analysis.

Given the costly investment in the necessary hardware and software, it sometimes seemed that authorities were reluctant to change to a different system of data collection and evaluation and would rather employ the computer firm who designed the packages to make the necessary adjustments. This was often a long drawn out process, and is one of the reasons why local authorities were slow in ascertaining the extent of need and in using other sets of figures important to the planning and targeting of services for children in need. One manager told the researchers:

> We have no proper data collection system but the social services has hired the research manager in the chief executive's dept. to do work on children. We recognise that the establishment of a management

information system for the establishment of the Community Care Act will have a beneficial knock-on effect on establishing a similar system for children.

Finally, it was suggested by senior managers that staffing and time allowed for analysis of data and subsequent dissemination for policy and planning were insufficient.

Identifying groups of children in need: some results

Section 17 intends that there should be a developmental link between the first two arms of need (a) and (b) and that disabled children should have the status of children in need by virtue of their disability.

Calculations undertaken by Bebbington and Miles (1989) of the likelihood of children entering the care system from disadvantaged socio-economic backgrounds would point to the value of promoting the welfare of children as outlined in arm (a). There is the possibility of a strong developmental link between children who come under arm (a) and those who are under arm (b). In other words a child could drift from being unlikely to achieve or maintain a reasonable standard of health or development into a child whose health or development would be likely to be significantly impaired. At the extreme this might mean that a child could be precipitated into being at risk of significant harm without the provision of family support services.

It is also the intention that disabled children should be included as a category in their own right in arm (c). This alone should be grounds for considering services. It is in theory possible for disabled children to also be placed in (a) or (b) if this is warranted by their circumstances.

It was clear that social services departments found the development of such links difficult to grasp. Respondents in the questionnaire had found it difficult to place predetermined groups of children within the three arms. This was explored further in interview and was confirmed as being problematic. One team leader summed up the difficulties:

> We have spent a lot of time discussing this. Sometimes it seems as not to square with the resources available to provide services. Therefore we have had to simply develop risk categories not necessarily based on any county data but on our own judgements.

In the case of children with disabilities, a total of 51 authorities (62%) assigned the children under arm (c), though not exclusively so; 21 authorities (26%) assigning children to arms (a), (b) and (c). One would have thought that all authorities would have at least placed disabled children under arm (c) given the comprehensive and unambiguous definition of disabled children in the Act. Even more surprisingly, 26 authorities (32%) did not recognise disabled children as a pre-determined group.

In the light of this it was decided to dispense with the distinction between arms (a), (b) and (c) of the definition in relation to exploring whether predetermined groups were used in identifying the extent of need and to collapse answers under the following two headings for predetermined groups:

1 Children for whom social services already have some responsibility; and

2 Children in the community

There was a considerable discrepancy between the frequency of those predetermined groups for children for whom social services already had responsibility and those in the community as Tables 2 and 3 show (pages 68 and 69).

As might be expected, the most popular pre-determined group was children at risk of significant harm, 62 out of 82 authorities (76%), closely followed by those at risk of neglect 61 (74%) and those in care 60 (73%), children accommodated 59 (72%) and children on remand 57 (70%). Care leavers also had a high profile, perhaps reflecting the new emphasis ascribed to this group in the Act under Section 24. By contrast, children in hospital were allocated to groups by less than half the authorities (33 authorities only). As suggested in Chapter 4, it may be that social services have not fully recognised their new responsibilities in relation to these children. Similarly, privately fostered children had low priority.

By contrast, a smaller number of pre-determined groups were used for children in the community. As Table 3 shows (page 69), only children with special educational needs 45 (55%), those disabled 56 (68%), children at risk of involvement in crime 40 (49%) were regarded as predetermined groups by around half the respondents. The lowest score was for children in independent schools, 6 social services departments (7%), using this predetermined group to ascertain the extent of need, and the highest was for disabled children 56 (68%) social services departments. The mid-spread of scores was between 30 and 35, for example, children at risk of being HIV positive 33 (40%), and those who had carers with disabilities 32 (39%) and those who had difficult family relationships 33 (40%) of local authorities using these predetermined groups to ascertain the extent of need in their area.

Given the powerful research evidence on the association between a background of low income, poor housing and single parenthood and the likelihood of entering the care system, not to mention low educational attainment (Heath et al. 1989) and poor health (see Department of Health 1991a), it was of some concern that children from homeless families 29 (35%), drug/solvent abusing children 27 (33%), children excluded from school 24 (29%), children in bed and breakfast accommodation 24 (29%), children with a mentally ill carer 23 (28%), children in substandard housing 22 (27%), children in low income families 22 (27%), and young people in bed and breakfast accommodation 22 (27%) were ascribed to a predetermined group by just over a quarter of local authorities. As will be shown in Chapter 4, the pattern of these initial designations for predetermined groups was reflected to a large extent in decisions about who should be eligible for priority services. The findings on pre-determined groups also echo the range of child categories cited on the policy documents. Additionally, interviews with managers confirmed that there was a clear weighting towards child protection and neglect. It would be wrong not to include these children but, as suggested above, these decisions were sometimes not made on the basis of Children Act driven data collection but rather on what had been seen as traditional high risk categories.

Further analysis on a regional basis revealed no discernible differences in the use of predetermined groups. The pattern nationally was mixed, reflecting the bias towards children for whom social services already had responsibility.

To a great extent, the initial phase of identifying pre-determined groups of children for ascertaining the extent of need is now past. But the message from the responses to the question relating to this aspect of implementation is that well-structured plans for data collection may have been absent in many cases, and that too much reliance might have been placed on inadequate sets of data and that sometimes, groups may have been designated on the basis of necessary services rather than on the basis of careful and wide-based planning.

Summary

This chapter has shown that planning styles for the initial stages of Children Act implementation varied. At one end there was wide consultation with elected members, other agencies and, occasionally users. At the other, there was a policy formulation executed by a small Children Act planning group without wide consultation or, in some cases, the use of extensive and reliable data.

Lack of personnel resources and technical inefficiency in data collecting and collating caused major problems although the will to engage in such an exercise in relation to ascertain need was evident.

Far higher priority was given to groups of children for whom the local authority already had some responsibility. Although a minority had clearly extended their range of categories to take account of new legislative demands, such as the under 8s, children with disabilities or care leavers, around two thirds did not place in predetermined groups those whom research has indicated may be at risk in the community, including child truants, children living in substandard conditions and those from low income families.

Chapter 3

Working Across the Organisational Divide

IN RECOGNITION of the fact that children may well have problems that do not come within the remit of social services alone, the Children Act requires local authorities to adopt a corporate strategy in the delivery of their services to children. "Corporateness" embraces the idea that there should be co-operative work done on behalf of **children in need** by various departments within a local authority. Work in this area should not therefore rest entirely on social services though in practice they would usually take a leading co-ordinating role. The Regulations and Guidance sum up the expectations of co-operation across the organisational divide:

> Sections 17(5), 27, 28 and 30 provide duties and powers in relation to co-operation between and consultation with different authorities including social services, education departments and housing authorities, health authorities and independent organisations.
>
> *(Regulations and Guidance vol 2, Department of Health, 1991, p.3)*

Further, there is the expectation that to translate the law into practice, local authorities will wish to develop a corporate policy and clear departmental procedures in respect of inter-departmental collaboration [to] ensure good co-operation at all levels. Effective co-operation between social services departments and other local authority departments implies the need for good and extensive planning and consultation. Considerable progress has been made on inter-departmental collaboration in child protection investigation, spearheaded by the comprehensive guidance in ***Working Together under the Children Act 1989, A Guide to Arrangements for Inter-Agency Co-operation for the Protection of Children from Abuse, (Department of Health 1991c).*** The brief of this study was to explore the extent of consultation in relation to Children Act implementation in general over and above any specific pooling of data in relation to ascertaining the extent of need.

Definitions of consultation

In order to explore the national picture at the stage of planning for implementation of the Act, six areas of consultation were investigated:

- meetings within social services
- meetings within local authorities with other departments;
- meetings with other agencies;
- documents distributed within social services;
- documents distributed within local authorities to other departments;
- documents distributed among agencies outside a local authority.

The study explored the extent to which social services had consulted through meetings with sections of the social services department, with other local authority departments, with other statutory agencies and with the voluntary sector. Enquiries were also made as to whether the contribution made in these liaisons was thought by the social services to be positive.

Similar explorations were made in respect of the circulation of consultation documents. The aim was to investigate the range and spread of organisations consulted. Comparisons were made between different regions and between metropolitan authorities and shires on the grounds that differences in political, socio-economic, geographical, and demographic structure might have a bearing on social services policy.

The framework for collaboration

In order to embark on any process of consultation, it is necessary to have channels of communication and a structure for action.

It was clear from the interviews with mangers that, as in the process of ascertaining need, consultation between social services and others for the purpose of Children Act implementation often depended upon good working relationships prior to the Act. In five of the interview authorities, the ascertaining of need had been a joint effort with different departments pooling their data to provide a joint data base, very much in the spirit the Act seemed to imply. Senior managers gave a positive response on this issue. In their authorities, there had often been the involvement of other agencies in the data collection process and the establishment of a definite relationship between the social services department and other agencies in the sharing of planning and distribution of information. Similarly, the Children Act implementation group had used well-established channels of communication with individuals to circulate policy documents and consult about policy and priorities of service delivery.

By contrast, without a foundation of good relationships, consultation was more superficial or was difficult to achieve. The other five senior managers said that there were few established channels for a shared data base with health, housing or education, for example. Meetings had been difficult to organise and were not well-attended. At the time of the interviews old barriers still existed, as exemplified by this senior officer:

> We've always had problems with Health and Education. There is good will on our side but everyone is scared that collaboration of any sort will have financial implications. In the past we have spent a lot of time haggling over who is to pay for a special residential placement - us or education. It is going to take a long time to change things. We just decided to develop our own policies.

It was normal for social services whose experience of consultation over data and services was positive to have established consultative committees to focus upon the sharing of data for Children Act implementation. One county, well advanced in its collaboration strategy, reported its process thus:

> It has been our intention to re-do our consultation process in relation to the data collection exercise and to plan policy and service delivery. We also have a consultation link between the client groups and the provider group, for instance between care leavers and housing. This acts as a feedback and monitoring mechanism. From this we can adjust to all kinds of data we collect ... whether we are gathering the right kind of data in relation to the problems that arise.

It was also clear from some of the research respondents that the voluntary sector was sometimes involved at the data collection stage and the planning stage. Three managers stated that they maintained ongoing data collection relationships with agencies such as the Children's Society and National Children's Homes whom they also used as providers of services.

This pattern was however not the norm. It was more likely that social services used various agencies as a data source for consultation on an ad hoc basis. Additionally, few authorities seemed to be beyond a beginning stage of formal consultation with the voluntary agencies in relation to the Children Act. While it was recognised by interviewees that voluntary agencies could offer useful information for planning, it was comparatively rare for this to have been included in evidence relating to the ascertaining of need. Many local authorities did not have the research infrastructure to make proper use of the products of consultation, as suggested in Chapter 2.

Range of Consultation

Earlier research by the Social Services Inspectorate (SSI 1992) had noted that, in London, consultation had been 'patchy'. In order to place this result from London in a national framework, consultation was compared within the various regions up and down the country (divisions made using Department of Health listings of regions) and between metropolitan boroughs and counties. Table 4 (page 70) shows the number of social services departments who had held consultation meetings within the social services department as well as with other local authority departments, and with other statutory and voluntary agencies.

As Table 4 (page 70) shows, for the most part the average across all regions was running to about just over 4 organisations with only the South West showing wide consultation which otherwise would skew the picture. Caution should be maintained in interpreting these figures - the South West appears to score highly, but this is on the basis of two local authority responses out of a possible six. So, for this reason, the South West is rather unrepresentative. If consultation is broken down by metropolitan and shire authorities, the average number of consulted organisations for metropolitan authorities was 4.6, and 4.1 for shire authorities (table not shown).

The first conclusion to be drawn from these two results is that in local authorities across the country the numbers of organisations consulted was generally between four and five. However, this comparatively low range for consultation was not the whole picture.

Table 5 (page 71) shows the number of social services who had consulted at least one of the relevant agencies and reveals that there was, as might be expected, a high rate of consultation with education 74 (90%), health 70 (85%) and housing 60 (73%) and a reasonable rate with leisure and recreation 48 (58%) but slightly less with the police 40 (49%) and the probation service 41 (50%). What is surprising was the lack of consultation meetings within social services themselves 36 (44%). Senior managers suggested in interview that the reason for this might have been the different organisational arrangements. Some very senior social services managers were more democratic than others.

This suggests an encouraging picture on the overall consultation between social services and others and shows that nationally, there was a fairly standard pattern of consultation. This result only gives a very broad picture; to obtain a more in depth picture of the extent of consultation within *each* authority, a more detailed investigation was then made of how many other local authority departments or outside agencies were consulted in meetings by social services.

Table 6 (page 72) shows that 12 social services departments (15%) did not consult any other departments or agencies but 38 (46%) consulted between 4 and 6 organisations. Wider consultation was rarer with only 16 social services departments (20%) having consulted between 7 and 14 other departments or agencies.

The results show that there was a fairly robust consultation process taking place both within and between different parts of the local authority and sometimes beyond with outside agencies like probation and the police.

To ascertain the extent of consultation with outside agencies, and to obtain the number of authorities who had consulted beyond the defined organisations set out in Sections 27 and 28 of the Children Act, the data was controlled for education, health and housing departments.

With this control operating just under half 39 (48%) of the 82 social services had at least consulted health, education and housing, and 41 (50%) social services had consulted health, education and housing, and at least one other department or agency.

It is clear from our interviews that social services had been developing their consultation processes over the 1992-93 period. If the national survey were to be repeated, there might be a reasonable increase in the extent of consultation presented here, although some traditional barriers could still be preventing a more collaborative approach in general.

Consultation for specific purposes

The extent of consultation meetings presented above may give a rosy picture of a burgeoning corporate identity in many local authorities and a strong interest in a general expansion of a mixed economy of welfare. With one exception, there was, however, no way of knowing in detail from the national survey about the purpose of meetings, only that they took place. There were clear indications from interview respondents that for the most part, consultation with others had taken place for the purpose of undertaking specific tasks, for example, discussing with the police how child protection procedures should be implemented or how social services and the health authority might co-operate over family support. It was however possible to test out the extent of collaboration in relation to one important development introduced in the Children Act - the joint register of disabled children.

Register of disabled children

The Act lays down a wide range of statutory provisions concerning disabled children not least of which is the requirement that local authorities will maintain a register of disabled children (Schedule 2, para. 2). In connection with registration, Guidance and Regulations emphasises that local authorities, in collaboration with health authorities, local education authorities, and voluntary agencies need to publicise widely the existence and purpose of registers to:

'. . . facilitate collaboration in identification and a co-ordinated provision of services under the (Children) Act.'

(Guidance and Regulations, vol 6, p.7).

Managers and team leaders consistently said that social services maintained good relations with both health and education in relation to disabled children. In 6 of the 10 authorities interviewed, users' groups had been involved. This was the one area where collaboration had often been long-standing both with regard to planning and service delivery. The extent of collaboration was confirmed by the postal survey where over two thirds of social services departments had reached agreement with others on the criteria for registration of disabled children. As Table 7 (page 73) shows, 50 departments (61%) had made agreements by the time of the study and of these 47 (57%) had been with at least both health and education. A third 27 (33%) had, however, not yet established criteria.

Three of the authorities interviewed had set up joint working parties for the purpose of establishing common criteria on a fairly formal basis. It must be remembered that for some social services who do not share boundaries with health authorities, this is a considerable exercise as they have to liaise with more than one authority. One of the interviewees reported that their county linked with five different health authorities. To have achieved a common criteria in this case seemed impressive.

It was evident that these traditional and complicated boundaries between county councils, and district and borough councils had inhibited the sharing of information and co-operation in general. In some cases, even though joint consultative committees had been set up for general Children Act consultation and planning, members from other parts of local government in other areas were reported to be reluctant participants. It was beyond the scope of the study to ascertain how widespread this problem was, but it seems worthy of further investigation.

Circulation of documents for consultation

The second area of consultation explored was the circulation of documents. It could be argued that the written dissemination of ideas for policy was an important part of the whole collaborative process towards implementation. Table 8 (page 74) shows that the circulation of documents mirrored the process of consultation through meetings, the highest scores relating to education, 65 out of 82 (79%), health 55 (67%) and housing 53 (65%). In several cases, circulation scores exceeded those of consultation meetings. But from a series of cross tabulations of consultation by circulation (not shown), it was evident that the rule was broadly that if local authorities were 'circulating', they were also 'consulting'.

Some examples of this were education, where out of 74 respondents (90%) who said they had consulted other agencies, 63 (77%) had held meetings and had circulated documents. For housing, out of 60 (73%) of social services departments who had consulted others. 47 (57%) had held meetings and had circulated documents. Finally, for health, out of 70 (85%) departments both 'consulting' and 'circulating', 52 (63%) had consulted and circulated documents. This is an encouraging sign in that it suggests that many local authorities were taking a two pronged approach which could only help to amplify and consolidate the consultation process, as well as increasing awareness of the Children Act policy agenda. Although it is beyond the scope of the data to be certain about any links between policy formation and policy dissemination, it is possible, from the connections between meetings and the widespread use of the written word, to speculate that this is a hypothesis worth testing.

The involvement of users

Though designed to elicit information on the consultation process between professionals, the postal questionnaire had left space for other consultants to be included. Rarely was this section completed and there was little indication of who these 'others' might be. In the interviews, the matter of user involvement in consultation was persued.

It seemed that there had been little involvement of users at the initial planning stage with the exception of the parents of disabled children. One of the interviewed social service departments had arranged meetings with well-established groups of parents who, prior to the Act had been involved in the development of respite services for their children. There had also been meetings in this authority with parents in family centres.

In general, working with user groups seemed more like an aspiration of the back of planners' minds than an ongoing reality. When pressed to list the groups, very few names were forthcoming other than MENCAP and other well-known nationally based organisations. Where consultations had taken place, it was more often the case that documents had been circulated to local groups as opposed to holding consultation meetings with them. Three team leaders were especially concerned that user group consultation had been tokenistic. Interviewees concluded that this layer of consultation had hardly begun but all believed it should happen. One stumbling block was the diversity of local issues; another was the lingering philosophy of service led planning.

Usefulness of the consultation process

Respondents in the postal survey were asked how they rated the consultation process on a three point scale. The results are shown in Table 9. As might be expected with such a blunt research instrument, 'acceptable' was the preferred response among those who completed this question. But the ratio by which the 'acceptable' responses outweigh the other possible responses is perhaps indicative of a *developing* relationship between one department and another with health clearly being the front runner for excellent relationships. Equally clear was the fact that consultation with the police was regarded as generally poor with half the social services departments (41) saying they had found the consultation process unsatisfactory. There were no indications of why this was so and the interview sample were untypical in this respect with several having established excellent relations with the police in relation to child protection investigations.

Finally, the study attempted to make some tentative links between consultation through meetings, circulation of documents and service provision. It might be that a wider and more trenchant consultation process would indicate a greater breadth of service provision by the social services in partnership with others. Even after extensive analysis, no distinct association was found between these three elements. The numbers of services provided by social services is relatively constant across local authorities whereas the number of agencies consulted or to whom documents were circulated varies from authority to authority. There seems to be no correlation either, between outside agencies who were consulted and whether they were used to provide services. It would appear that the consultation/document circulation process and the spread of the mixed economy of provision are separate processes. However, it is still comparatively early days in the implementation of the Act. Both the policy documents and the interviews with managers suggest that many successful partnerships between agencies often pre-existed the Act.

Summary and conclusions

Overall, there is much to be applauded with regard to the links established between social services and other agencies and departments. The basic strategy of consulting and circulating, and of satisfying statutory duties seemed to be in place for many local authorities at the end of September 1993.

In terms of corporateness and co-ordination, social services had succeeded in making positive links between health, housing, education, and social services. There were, at the time of the study, few links with planning and transport departments, and from the policy documents, it seems that only a handful of authorities took these departments into account. Additionally, the relationship with the police was varied, and the probation service had a lower profile than might be expected.

What was also missing were wider links with other agencies on a strategic basis such as voluntary agencies, from interviews and policy documents, it is clear that authorities recognised the need to consult more widely and were continuing to develop this.

There is evidence that in some cases links had been forged for specific purposes rather than to develop an overall corporate strategy.

Two thirds of local authorities had succeeded in adopting common criteria for registration of disabled children.

From the results presented, there are several implications for policy:-

- It would seem from the interviews, that social services successes in consultation were based on the strength of *existing* relationships with various organisations pre-Act. To continue to reinforce such good relationships will be essential for future development.
- Continuation of the efforts by social services to extend their range of consultation should be encouraged, and there should be more examination of the forms that it takes both in terms of who is consulted, and how formalised and structured are the processes to ensure an ongoing commitment to corporate activity.
- There is a need for monitoring, to ensure that the consultation process is not merely cursory.

Chapter 4

Deciding priorities for service provision

WHILE ALL local authorities are expected to ascertain the needs of children in their area, it is clear that the Act intends this information as a data base from which decisions can be made about service delivery.

> Local authorities are not expected to meet every individual need, but they are expected to identify the extent of need and then make decisions on the priorities for service provision in their area in the context of that information and their statutory duties.
>
> *(Regulations and Guidance, Department of Health, vol 2, p.7)*

It might be expected that in reaching decisions about priorities, local authorities would take account of their data bases, however inadequate these were. It could also be a reasonable expectation that they would take into account information from the increasingly fertile resource of research studies in social work, health and education which have pointed to those circumstances which render some children highly at risk both of significant harm and of their development being impaired (see for example, Bradshaw 1990). Nor would it be unreasonable to expect that studies on the potential negative outcomes of growing up in care, see *Department of Health and Social Security (1985) and Department of Health (1991)*, would influence the will to provide services to prevent family breakdown for children who might be defined as a priority for service provision. To condense this breadth of information and link it to groups of children in a particular locality, it was considered helpful to develop two main headings for predetermined groups of children who potentially could be eligible for high priority services:–

- those for whom social services already have some responsibility; and
- those in the community;

It was recognised that there might be a third source for determining priorities: i.e. referrals of individual children. Accordingly, in the postal survey, explorations were made along these three dimensions.

Children for whom social services departments already have responsibility

Under the first general heading of those children for whom social services departments already had some responsibility fell the following:

1 children in care

2 children accommodated

3 children at risk of significant harm or neglect

4 children in hospital for over 3 months

5 children privately fostered

6 young people who have left the care system

7 young people on remand into local authority care

Children in the community

Under this heading some obvious clusters of predetermined groups emerged, all of which have been given prominence in research on children.

1 family stability

2 housing problems

3 poverty

4 education

5 disabilities

6 ethnic minorities

7 deviance and delinquency

Tables 10 and 11 (pages 76 and 77) confirm the findings of the interim report and the findings in Chapter 2: in relation to predetermined groups to ascertain need, there was an overwhelming emphasis on giving priority to children for whom the local authority already had some responsibility. As Table 11 shows, with the exception of children in hospital and those privately fostered, around two thirds of authorities were giving priority to all groups under this heading. Children at risk of abuse and neglect, those accommodated or in care were ranked the highest. This is an identical ranking to the predetermined groups used to ascertain need reported in Table 2 (page 68).

Tuning to Table 12 (page 78), there are similar parallels with Table 3 (page 69).

Not surprisingly, therefore, low priority was accorded to many of the groups of children in the community who were in living conditions or were exhibiting behaviours that traditionally caused concern about health and development such as poverty, substandard housing, homelessness and truanting. These were only seen as groups eligible for priority service provision by a minority of social services departments. The same concerns expressed in Chapter 2 apply here: that the developmental link between promotion of welfare and risk of significant harm is being ignored.

Children with disabilities were the group within the community most likely to be given a high priority for services but only about half of social services departments, 44 (54%) said that disabled children as a predetermined group would be a high priority for services in spite of the fact that the Act cites disabled children as a group in need in their own right. In interview, it was clear for at least six authorities that disability *per se* would not automatically qualify a child for priority services. There might have to be some other 'risk' as well either under arm (a) or arm (b). This paradox was clearly exercising at least two of the team leaders interviewed. Their views echoed the current debate among policy makers as to whether disabled children are most appropriately regarded as a 'group apart' under arm (c) of Section 17 or whether their needs can be adequately met under one of the other two arms of need.

When enquiries were made about individual referrals, (with categories developed by the research team in collaboration with the Department of Health) as Table 13 (page 79) shows, a rather more solid picture emerged but one which still reflected a bias towards children at risk of abuse or neglect for whom the authority already has some responsibility. Individuals who were disabled were given a higher profile 63 (77%) than when disability was a predetermined group 44 (54%) as discussed above (see also Table 12, page 78). A child at risk because of behaviour problems or drug abuse was more likely to get priority as an individual referral than a child who had been designated to a predetermined group for these reasons. Those living in circumstances that might place stress on families such as a child in a low income family were also likely to be given priority services if referred. Children who were homeless or those living in poor housing conditions were less likely to be given a high priority for service as were children designated to predetermined groups for these reasons.

Such results were disturbing and to some extent puzzling since there is a clear expectation in the Act that the three arms of need would allow for a model of service provision that recognises the interface between developmental issues and risk. Additionally, it had been made quite cleat to local authorities in Guidance and Regulations that to confine services to children at risk of significant harm would be illegal (Department of Health 1991b, para. 2.4).

There could be a variety of reasons for the infrequent use of priority groups to determine services and the narrower approach than might be expected to using characteristics of children referred as individuals as a base for decisions.

1 It could be that social services were finding it difficult to move from a social policing role to a more balanced support role for children.

2 Social services might also be finding it difficult to move from a service led role to one that was based on data and ascertained need.

3 In relation to disabled children, it might be that local authorities were still in the process of developing services on a planned inter-agency basis as recommended in Regulations and Guidance.

> Many children with disabilities will require support from a very wide range of services. Their need for services will often be a continuing need. An ongoing process of assessment, monitoring and review will therefore be essential in order to ensure appropriateness and effectiveness of service provision . . . Since the development of individual packages of care will necessitate negotiation . . . across a wide range of agencies, a team base for such an arrangement may be the most effective.
>
> *(Regulations and Guidance, Department of Health, 1991d, vol 6, p.11).*

4 The Act introduced new requirements in respect of children in hospital and those privately fostered. Could it be that local authorities were not clear or adequately prepared for these new responsibilities?

5 The period of implementation of the Children Act had coincided with the introduction of three other major pieces of legislation which had implications for the concept of parental responsibility. Could this have blurred the very clear definition in the Children Act?

6 The low overall use of predetermined groups to set priorities for planning services could have been connected to the absence of certain large groups in individual authorities although, given the clear messages from research about the associations between socio-economic factors and admission to care (see Department of Health 1991a), these children would have been responded to favourably as individuals.

7 Given the embryonic development of shared data bases in relation to ascertaining need, it was likely that any planning for services based on the collection was slow in its development.

As suggested in Chapter 2, scrutiny of the policy documents of authorities provided evidence of variation in the range of priorities from many heavily focused towards child protection investigation to broad statements which had grasped the relationship between promotion of welfare and protection from significant harm but there were few clues about the evidence upon which these statements had been conceived. Only a handful, including one rural county, seemed to have thought through the implications for planning of a distinction between predetermined groups and individuals. This county made reference to the Social Services Inspectorate study *Capitalising on the Act (HMSO 1992)* in its policy statement and recognised that one need, say relating to education, might be linked to another, say relating to health or family situation.

One metropolitan borough stood out in having developed a sophisticated matrix which linked groups of children to implementation strategy, operational goals and indicators. Their strategy showed clearly how prioritisation might revolve, not around individual children but around the objectives stated in the Act. It then related these to service provision. Child protection is defined widely: the protection of children from both the harm which can arise from failures in the family or abuse *and* from the harm which can be caused by unwarranted intervention in their family life. The operational goals then set out how these twin objectives can be satisfied by providing a broad range of services.

The most common thread evident in the policy documents was that it was acceptable to lay down firmly the boundaries of potential service delivery. That a child fell into one of the predetermined groups for ascertaining need did not entitle him or her automatically to be a priority for a service.

These issues were taken up with senior managers and team leaders in order to inquire in more depth into the base upon which priority services were being offered.

Their responses helped to clarify several important issues.

The emphasis on child abuse investigation and a mistaken definition of statutory responsibilities

Firstly, both senior managers and team leaders unanimously were of the opinion that the term 'statutory duties' referred *only* to cases for which the local authority already had some responsibility. At least half went further and said they defined statutory responsibilities as those involving the protection of children from abuse. A typical comment from a team leader was:

> As far as I can see, we have a very clear boundary between services we have to offer and those that are optional. Obviously, we have to deal with child abuse referrals but if another comes in to ask for help with her marital problems we are not interested. We simply haven't the time. It's a great shame.

Another team leader said:

> I've been in child care social work for 25 years but I am taking early retirement. Morale is really low. We are told - only deal with statutory cases, child abuse and offenders. I thought it would be better after the Children Act but it is worse. It is silly because I know from experience that you need to work with the families over a period of time.

Another said:

> We are just police. It's no wonder the public doesn't like social workers. I can see the need to follow up families after investigation but we are not allowed to do so. It's all statutory work.

And another:

> Education welfare do all the support work these days. We refer children back to them if there isn't going to be a court case or statutory investigation. That would have been unheard of a few years ago.

There were two exceptions to the boundaries between investigative work and support but even here the echo was of 'them and us'. One team leader of a children and families team in a busy city office said:

> At the moment we are managing to ring fence some preventive services like respite care as well as statutory services. It's the only way. The Children Act has given me clout to push support services. Before it was all child abuse investigation. Now we get field social workers coming to my team asking us to take on a family where there is some risk. If we get in early, sometimes we can prevent a crisis.

Such a mistaken definition of Section 17 and such a prescriptive approach helps to explain partially the weighting out of answers in the national questionnaire towards children for whom the local authority already had responsibility and the heavy emphasis on child protection investigation. It was also clear that, in a world of finite resources, choices had been made to cover the work that was most pressing. To put it bluntly, as did one senior manager: 'No one wants a dead child on their caseload'.

The emphasis on investigation and lack of accompanying support services reported here is confirmed by the recently completed Department of Health funded study into the early investigative process in child sex abuse cases by Jones et al. (1993). Parents whose investigations had been closed told researchers in that study of their concerns about being 'dropped' without the offer of further help. But more importantly, there was evidence that children's recovery from investigations without remedial or supportive services in these circumstances was slow.

A service or needs led definition of need

Most of the managers interviewed confirmed the response to the questionnaire: that the use of predetermined groups based on data to establish priority services for children in the community was not widely used, with the exception of disabled children and one or two other groups mentioned in the Act, such as youngsters leaving care. There was, however, some positive evidence about the development of needs led as opposed to service led priority provision, although it seemed to be developing in not quite the way the Act intended. In many cases decisions about service priority groups had been made by the implementation group described in Chapter 2. There were three main approaches:

The first (in line with the Act) was to undertake a proper survey of need and then target priority groups accordingly. A principal officer in a large county with a well-developed corporate approach said:

> When we did our sums with health and education, we realised how behind we were with children with disabilities, Given the Act says they are children in need by definition and that we had so many, we put a lot of money into improving services. Parents were involved in decisions. We have increased the budget for these children five-fold but we had a lot to catch up on.

The second approach was to simply take the children highlighted in the Act as a priority group irrespective of the local situation.

A senior manager said:

> One of the central messages of the Act we identified at the planning stage was the importance of 'leaving care' issues, and we followed this through at the stage of prioritization.

The third approach was to define need along three dimensions, high medium and low risk, based not on data or research evidence but on traditional criteria for allocating children to these groups intuitively.

This authority was using the 'traditional' definition of primary, secondary and tertiary prevention. To be fair to the authority, they were clearly basing their levels of 'risk' on sound empirical work and standard sociological definitions of prevention: (see, for example, Hardiker et al. 1991b):

> We felt that we had to know some of the basic grids which had appeared in the literature we knew, and using a three level model was common as well as giving us an obvious way to define priorities. We could always refine it later on.

Several authorities used an alternative model of three levels, which was service led. There was a first level which referred to an advisory role for the authority which helped children and families make their own arrangements or links with services elsewhere or through open access points such as family centres within the authority itself. The second level involved professional help in support of the child and family for the protection of the child where there had been a risk assessment. The third level called for 'heavy end' intervention using powers to protect the child and provide accommodation or care.

There were dangers in adopting this approach which imposed a 'gate structure' on some families to divert resources to the third level. The idea of levels was in itself problematic and in danger of resurrecting old boundaries such as those between care in the community and accommodation, for example. One team leader thought that as a result of this model there might be a lot of unmet need because families lacked the skills to negotiate services for themselves.

Whatever approach was taken, there were some gaps in implementing new requirements, such as those for children in hospital. One or two senior managers were vague about the requirement while the team leaders were also uncertain and worried about the imposition of yet another responsibility on an already hard-pressed team in the absence of additional resources. Such constraints confirm the finding in the postal survey that little attention was being given to this group of children.

Barriers to implementing a needs led priorities for service provision

Finally, it was clear that barriers to the development of a service based on data-led priority need had been imposed by several constraints. There were traditional often rigid boundaries between agencies and a fear that social services would have to fund new developments.

A senior manager:

> The elected representatives agreed with the [priority groups] as long as voluntary organisations didn't get any more money . . . there was a lot of bloodletting in the social services because everyone wanted to do everything and represent their group of children, leaving care, under fives etc. collaborative work can cause a lot of pain to a lot of people . . . they may not always have all the answers.

This particular response highlighted the reality of the carving up of a small cake between various teams. Each team in this authority was vying with another to show how *their* data and judgement could make *their* children deserving of being a priority group for services. There was little evidence of overall management of this process. The bickering was reminiscent of social workers in case conferences in Hallet and Stevenson's study over a decade ago who were described as rivals rather than as a team (Hallet and Stevenson 1980).

It was clear that in some authorities there had been extensive Children Act training in 1991 but that this had not been continued because of the anticipation of the Community Care Act. It was a message of 'We did the Children Act then we had to move on to prepare for the Community Care'. As a result, the complex messages of the Act in relation to Section 17 sometimes seemed to have been ill-digested.

Community care had also brought in its wake complete reorganisation across the whole of social services. This was evident in one authority which had wrestled with the imposition of a purchaser -provider model on a comprehensive and interwoven child care service. The dilemma had been solved by ensuring that, at a senior level in children and families teams, experienced social workers could be both purchasers and providers so that family support could fit alongside child protection investigations. But it had been a hard battle to preserve such continuity.

Finally, the research respondents confirmed the inadequate infrastructure for handling and pulling together diverse information. Attempts to estimate priority groups had been abandoned in two cases because of the difficulties of gaining accurate information. Managers had thought it more reliable to base priorities on a retrospective count of referrals.

Summary and conclusions

Interviews with senior and middle managers confirmed the findings of the interim report: that too much emphasis is still being given to child protection investigation at the expense of family support services.

There is a fundamental misunderstanding of the meaning of statutory responsibility under Section 17 which warrants more guidance from central government.

The fear of a child abuse scandal influences the dominance of this work at the expense of supportive services where there are finite resources.

Priority for service provisions is often being calculated on the basis of referrals with less evidence of comprehensive forward planning based on local data and research evidence. Personnel interviewed confirmed confusion about the intention of the Act in this area.

Family support services are often seen as optional and a luxury rather than as an integral part of Section 17 services, thereby helping to exclude children in need in the community who have not yet become the responsibility of social services.

Finally, decisions about priority groupings may be influenced by fiscal pressures and by the relative power of different interest groups. One policy officer summed up the complexities of the implementation process in relation to priority service decisions:

> This was a delicate process. We had to involve members, users, voluntary agencies and various members of social services teams. We sometimes found that we had to be more concerned with 'keeping the show on the road' than with firm decision making. This was further complicated by the split between users and specialised agencies wanting what was best for their groups, social services officers trying to base decisions on what we knew about the extent of need, and the social services committee members wanting to make decisions on the basis of political or ideological issues and financial control.

There are important implications for policy guidance from this chapter:

- That statutory duties are not confined to investigation of child abuse;
- That more guidance needs to be given on the essential relationship between protection and family support: support services are necessary not optional in order to achieve the aims of the Act.
- The significance and consequences for service priority of disabled children being a category in their right in Section 17 warrant more explanation. There is confusion about the circumstances under which disabled children might be a priority for services.

Chapter 5

Service Delivery and the Mixed Economy of Welfare

Introduction

THIS CHAPTER addresses the implementation of Section 17 in respect of service provision. Traditionally family support services have been equated with a social services, if not a social work approach, even if the social services department has had a long-standing partnership with voluntary child care agencies to whom it has delegated some of its responsibilities in respect of specific provisions, such as, residential care or family centres. The Children Act now places an emphasis upon services being delivered by a wider range of agencies which should routinely include both voluntary as well as statutory agencies.

> In putting together packages of services, local authorities should take account of services provided by the voluntary sector and other agencies
>
> *(Guidance and Regulations, Department of Health, vol. 2, HMSO 1992 p.8)*

Section 27 of the Children Act requires a corporate approach to service provision between education, health housing and other authorised persons. Partnership is thus given a much broader meaning - partnership between potential providers as well as between purchasers and providers.

Extent of provision of services

As Table 14 (page 80) shows, most local authorities claim to be providing most of the services listed in the national questionnaire. Where there is a shortfall, the majority of local authorities said they were planning to develop missing services or improve on existing services (table not shown). Table 15 (page 81) shows that for only a few services do the scores fall below 55%, eg. laundry, education for children looked after who are not attending day school, holiday activities, and helping children and families to holidays. So in terms of provision of services in each local authority, there is a wide selection of services **available**. Statistical analysis suggested that there were no distinct patterns according to region or type of authority. It was beyond the scope of the postal questionnaire to ascertain the scale of provision within each of these services but those interviewed indicated that there might be a variation in provision and that in some services a shortfall would be expected. There was a wide range of Section 17 payments, for example. One county provided family centres only in its two major towns. The officer interviewed was concerned about the shortfall of rural provision.

> Take family centres – yes we have several mostly open access ones because that is our policy but it is worrying that they are located unevenly within the county. We are not sure how to solve this. Should we have a play bus type of provision which travels around the villages? Or should we consider a private transport system to bring families into the towns, the bus service being so bad and too expensive for many of our families? We can't afford to reach everywhere.

It was also made clear in the interviews that many of these services were probably available and working well long before the Children Act, so that provision within the Act may reflect a continuity and development of services, (an approach which team leaders in particular thought helpful when they were arguing for their continuation).

How services are being provided

In order to explore how far local authorities had developed a **variety of means to provide services**, inquiries were made about the providers of each service. Table 15 (page 81) shows that there are fascinating sets of emergent patterns of provision arrangements. Earlier data in the interim report based on returns from 60 authorities produced an impression of social services departments as the dominant provider of services. This suggested that the involvement of other agencies and departments was somewhat sparse. The data from the revised sample of 82 requires a modest review of this impression, and points to the greater involvement of organisations other than the social services department in service provision. A brief look at the scores for the method-of-provision across a range of services in Table 15 suggests that, social services still dominates provision, (with few other methods of provision coming up to half the number of voluntary agencies) and that there is a developing use of other local authority departments for specific services such as supervision for matrimonial cases. Private company provision remains negligible. Ad hoc purchase of service as a method of provision remains fairly unpopular.

In interview, both team leaders and senior managers suggested that the ad hoc purchase or private arrangement is not necessarily a good method of provision in that it is inherently unstable with regard to continuity of a particular type of service. Such an arrangement might breakdown due to budget difficulties or to failure by the provider. Additionally, there was concern about quality control of both private and ad hoc services.

Turning to the question of who is providing what, and focusing on the combination of providers providing any one service, it becomes clear, that the picture is very mixed. The data conveys the complexity of the current arrangements nationally, a feature confirmed in interviews with managers.

Four examples of mixed economy services

Perhaps the best way to illustrate the variety and complexity of a developing mixed economy of provision is to single out four services. In this way, it is possible to see, for instance, how many authorities were using only social services to provide, say, family centres, as against how many authorities were offering family centres using social services, voluntary agencies, and another local authority department. Tables 16-19 (pie charts) explore the extent to which the service provision relates to the *method* of provision.

Family Centres

Family Centres have a high profile in Children Act requirements for local authorities. They were a familiar feature of the child care family support provision before 1989, and existing research shows them to be provided by both local authorities and voluntary organisations see for example Smith (1992). In addition, they appear to represent a particularly flexible framework within which to deliver Part III services.

From Table 16 (see page 82), it can be seen that, across the 82 authorities who responded to the questionnaire, the predominant patterns were provision by social services 27 (33%) and by a combination of social services and voluntary organisations 24 (29%). The two other significant patterns of provision are by voluntary organisations 11 (13%) and 'other combinations' 13 authorities (16%).

The conclusion to be drawn from this complex pattern is that, the dominant mode of provision, remains with social services, either alone or in partnership with the voluntary sector. Together these constitute just over three quarters (76%) of authorities providing family centres. Thus in the matter of family centres, the 'mixed economy' approach is shared between social services and voluntary agencies.

Out of School Care

By comparison with family centres, many of whose services are directed toward children under 5, out of school care is by definition provided for children who are for the most part 5 years and older. Unlike family centres, parental attendance is rarely required, and out of school care underlines, of course, the relationship between social services departments and education authorities.

Table 17 (see page 85) shows the various means of provision of this service. The number of local authorities who are not providing out of school care at all is 7 (9%). There is no overall common pattern of service provision. In 13 authorities (16%) provision is by another LA department i.e. education. In 6 authorities, provision is by the voluntary sector. In 8 authorities, provision is jointly shared by social services and another local authority department. The majority pattern to emerge is 'other combinations' (54%) such as a voluntary organisation alongside education or leisure and recreation with either social services or education.

Unlike family centres, which are a well established service, out of school provision is a relatively new development. It is, therefore, perhaps not surprising that there is a greater variation in arrangements than the more traditional pattern which has emerged in respect of family centres. But such variation is interesting and suggests that a new service may attract a variety of service providers.

Respite Care

The Children Act extends the provision of short term accommodation for children to families in general as well as to children with disabilities who have already been offered this service in the past. Some would argue it is a particularly creative part of Section 17 duties (see, for example, Aldgate 1993). We examined the provision of both these types of respite service and observed whether any differences emerged between these two specific aspects of respite care. One very obvious difference became apparent: in the case of short term accommodation in general, social services departments appear to 'monopolise the delivery of services'. By comparison, in provision of short-term accommodation for disabled children, social services appear as one service provider amongst several others.

It is beyond the scope of the data to identify the reasons for these differences. Ongoing work by Aldgate, Bradley and Hawley (at the Universities of Leicester and Oxford) on general respite care, suggests that short-term accommodation may often overtly be offered to families whose children may be in need, either under arm (a) or arm (b) of Section 17. This is an area which points the way towards further qualitative research in order to ascertain the relationship between particular family circumstances and the types of services which children and their families are offered. It is hoped that the current study by Aldgate, Bradley and Hawley will illuminate this issue.

In examining the figures it is helpful to contrast respite care for children in general (Table 18 on page 86) with that for children with disabilities (Table 19 on page 87).

In the case of general respite care, over half was provided by social services 45

(55%), the only significant alternative being a combination of social services and ad hoc arrangements 14 (17%). This is not surprising, since in many authorities, general respite seems to be linked to family placement provision or to specialist neighbourhood respite care teams (see Aldgate 1993).

There was quite a marked contrast between this and the provision of respite care for children with disabilities (see Table 18). Provision for children with disabilities was not dominated by social services alone, though they were present in nearly all patterns of provision. Only 27 social services departments (33%) offered respite themselves. Two other patterns of provision were also represented : social services *and* ad hoc arrangements 16 (20%) and social services *and* voluntary agencies 12 (15%). The next largest 'slice', 7 authorities (9%), represented the *combination* of social services, voluntary agencies and ad hoc arrangements.

Therefore, it looks as though there was the beginning of a 'mixed economy' in relation to services for children with disabilities, although social services were still involved as stake holders in many cases. By contrast, general respite care was firmly in the hands of social services.

Responses to the mixed economy of care

In the interviews, senior and middle managers were asked about social services' attitudes towards the mixed economy of care. There was a keen interest in understanding the differences or shared opinions on this issue as between elected members and officers. One might suppose that the responses of elected members might turn on political party and ideology, but the much greater emphasis now being placed on budgeting in local government, often renders such considerations obsolete. In their responses, senior mangers implicitly assumed that any difference of attitude between members and officers would in part be reflective of the broad ideological divide between those in favour and those against the facilitation by others of the provision of services. While managers grasped the possible political dimensions to varying attitudes, they themselves had a primary concern with continuity of policy, and were not inclined to take the view that necessarily it was social services, as a matter of principle, who should in most cases be responsible for the provision of most services. One manager noted that:

> There was no obvious difference even prior to April (when there was a change of control of the council). We continue to have a very positive approach to the mixed economy. It is regarded by members and officers as good value for money.

Others made comments such as:

> There was no opposition [to mixed economy] from politicians, the issue

> was how much money to spend on it;

and

> there were no significant differences between elected members from different parties

Where the policy toward mixed economy provision did change according to changes of the political party in control of the local authority, officers expressed frustration:

> We had a clear policy in favour of developing the contracting out of some services, now there has been a political change and elected members are saying "no" to the original policy. We are no longer clear as to what to do . . .

One officer from an authority which did not, by and large, endorse the idea of 'other providers' said there was no difference between members and officers, but went on to say:

> there has been no attempt to provide services by other means where those services have always been provided by social services.

This seems to be saying that only services relating to new duties under legislation will be considered for contracting out, a view which reflected the findings on out of school provision reported above. Although the interview sample is small and may not be representative, it is fairly clear that those interviewed were, for the most part concerned with continuity of policy, and elected members wanted efficiency and value for money, irrespective of political beliefs about 'provision by others'.

Subsequent questions were concerned with the specific evaluation of the statutory, voluntary, and private sectors as providers. There was general recognition that each sector had its part to play in delivering quality services. This was despite the fact that across all authorities private companies were little used. There was no particular pattern of response to these questions. Authorities varied in their views of what roles the three different sectors could best fulfil. One response indicative of a positive attitude towards the mixed economy of care was that:

> We take a pragmatic attitude . . . we ask two questions: What can they deliver? and Can they deliver?

Other responses were more specific such as, that the statutory sector would support families who were not attractive to the independent sector and provide residential care and family centres. This particular authority saw it as essential that the local authority took responsibility for registration and inspection. Two authorities saw the role of the statutory sector in terms of making assessments and a co-ordinating role in the provision of services. Interestingly, both these authorities made it clear that assessment was not confined to child protection or 'heavy end' assessment and both suggested that a residualist role for social services would be 'problematic'.

Views on the roles of voluntary agencies and of the private sector were similar. Among our interviewees some saw specialist services, support of the under 8s, and innovation in services as appropriate to the voluntary sector, and others, as appropriate to the private sector. There was agreement that both of these sectors performed a useful function in locating 'niches in the market'. Some stressed that the point was to ensure 'good service agreements and good partnerships'. In other words, that there had to be some means of quality control.

Some tentative conclusions may be drawn. The mixed economy of care is not usually seen as a 'political football', nor is it perceived as one more means of budgetary control. It tends to be seen as an opportunity to increase the quality of specialist services and to provide services which a statutory agency would not otherwise provide.

Service provision for disabled children

The Act lays down a wide range of statutory provisions concerning disabled children, not least of which are the requirements that local authorities provide suitable accommodation for disabled children (Section 23(8)); that a local authority may assess a disabled child's needs coinciding with assessment under other legislation; and, most importantly, that a local authority should provide services designed to minimise the effects of disability, and give those children the opportunity to live as normal a life as possible (Schedule 2 para. 9).

In the interviews we focused on several aspects of service provision relating to disabled children. Firstly, there was an exploration of whether disabled children were being dealt with under the Children Act or under the Community Care Act. All managers interviewed said they were acting under the provisions of the Children Act, though one authority said "both". This authority placed disabled children over 14 within adult services and made them subject to the Community Care Act.

Senior managers and team leaders were asked whether the Children Act definition of disability had led to an expansion of local authority responsibility for children with special needs. To this there was a most positive response. One officer pointed out that the Children Act had changed the basis on which disabled children were evaluated.

> Formerly we linked needs to specific diagnoses, we now look at general

problems of delayed development.

One county had experienced the most radical changes:

> We have had to build up our services from square one as health took most of the major initiatives. We did not know what were the problems of disabled children originally. This has meant that we have had to make a major investment.

The special emphasis placed on disabled children under the Act seems to have enhanced provision of services and budgets for them. The requirement to bear joint responsibility with others for agreeing criteria for the register may also be a means of establishing consultation procedures with other authorities and agencies in order to build up service provision, (although at the moment, any developments across boundaries seem to have grown out of existing provision and agency ways of working).

Publicity

It has been suggested both by research and by the various documents that led to the children Act (eg the Short Report 1984) that one of the concerns of the public is that information about services is difficult to access to understand. Under schedule 2, part 1, para. 2 local authorities have a duty to:

> publish information:
>
> about services provided by them under Sections 17, 18, 20 and 24; and

(a) where they consider it appropriate, about the provision by others . . . of services which the authority have power to provide under those Sections; and

(b) take such steps as are reasonably practicable to ensure that those who might benefit from the services receive the information relevant to them.

The Regulations and Guidance (vol. 2) expands on these points noting that:

> This means that local authorities should publish information about advice provided by others. (p.13)

Account should be taken of 'ethnic minorities' cultural and linguistic needs' and of those with sensory disabilities.

This is an area of policy which needs more research. From our interviews it seems likely that publicity efforts are not very far advanced. Most of the publicity mentioned was in pamphlet form and written in English. The materials were available in the expected places - schools, libraries, social services. One authority illustrated the attitude that "if you really need to know, you'll contact the social services department."

There were exceptions. One county's response was encouraging. They were currently 'spending money for improving dissemination ... employing new staff for the specific task of dissemination'. Apart from the opportunity to discuss issues with a social worker, they distribute widely leaflets (which are available in a number of languages), use other agencies in the dissemination process, and have prepared tapes for the visually impaired.

It was heartening that there was some evidence of strides forward in making services more accessible but there was an impression that the process had just begun.

Summary and conclusions

To conclude, social services provision still dominates but to a lesser extent than originally thought in the interim report. There is a move toward a 'mixed economy of care'. Nationally, there are no strong patterns of partnerships of provision across the range of services. There is a very varied picture.

The Act has had an impact on improving services for disabled children.

Chapter 6

Summary of the main findings and policy recommendations

THIS CHAPTER highlights some of the main findings from the study. Its purpose has been to provide a broad national picture of the range of approaches to implementing Section 17 adopted by social services departments in England. The data is based on the results of a postal questionnaire to all 108 authorities of whom 82 responded and on in depth interviews with senior and middle management in 10 local authorities. Early findings were included in Chapter 3 of ***Children Act 1989, A Report by the Secretaries of State for Health and for Wales on the Children Act 1989 in pursuance of their duties under Section 83(6) of the Act, (1992) Cm 2144 HMSO 1992***

The study investigated four main areas of implementation:–

- ascertaining the extent of need;
- working across the organisational divide;
- establishing priorities for services
- providing services.

Ascertaining the extent of need

The Act requires local authorities to take reasonable steps to ascertain the extent of need' in their area. This presented a major challenge to many authorities. To develop strategies for ascertaining need and implementing the Act in general, implementation groups of senior managers and policy officers at a high level were established by the majority of local authorities, some as early as 1989. Much of the basis work at this stage was done 'in house' by social services, although a minority of implementation groups did recruit members from education and health and involved elected members in the spirit of corporate enterprise outlined in the legislation. Some of these groups have now been disbanded but others retain a monitoring function.

Many local authorities approached the task of ascertaining need in their area with some trepidation. To some extent, this might have been due to an absence of computer - held records, inappropriate soft ware packages and a shortfall of staffing for a comprehensive data analysis of the extent of need. Technical problems did not explain all of the difficulties. It was clear both from the postal survey and the interviews that some authorities found the forward - looking notion of ascertaining need alien to previous monitoring of need which had been based on an overview of reasons for referrals over a set period rather than using more comprehensive data, including that from health and education, for example, to identify groups of children who could be in need.

There were exceptions: a minority of authorities used extensive demographic data to ascertain need, identifying groups of children likely to be in need in respect of location, age or health, for example. These groupings were then included in the policy documents spelling out the local interpretation of children in need. Although the initial exercise of ascertaining need is now past, the research suggests that it was done hastily in some authorities and that a triennial review of the data and the widening of that data base would be desirable to ensure that changing demographic variables are accounted for.

Working across the organisational divide

Although ascertaining the extent of need had been problematic, most social services departments had embraced the spirit of the Act to consult with other departments, both in relation to decisions about policy and service provision, in accordance with Section 27. Around half had consulted (either through documents or meetings) at least 4 other organisations, with health and education being the most popular. It was clear that in the early stages, existing good relationships between different agencies had provided a sound foundation from which to move to a more corporate approach, while the Children Act had given 'permission' for old barriers to be broken down. At the time of the interviews (summer 1993), consultation had widened to include voluntary agencies and user groups, and was ongoing. However, there still remains a distinction between developing a wider partnership in relation to a general corporate strategy for implementation of Section 17 and consultation on specific issues, such as the register for disabled children, with more authorities engaging in the latter at present.

Establishing priorities for services

Having ascertained the extent of need, the Children Act requires local authorities to make decisions on the priorities for service provision in the light of that information and their statutory duties.

Around half the local authorities had linked strategies for service provision to data derived from a combination of specific, locally defined pre-determined groups and information on individual referrals. Data reliability has varied considerably. There have been many technical problems associated with poor computing software, absence of good computer records and a dearth of personnel to collect and collate statistics.

A hierarchy of both need and access was evident. Many authorities determined priority service groups on the basis of problems which attracted a pre Children Act professional definition of 'high risk' rather than basing their priorities on empirical data about children who might be in need in their area. Traditional responsibilities also dominated service priorities with less than one third of authorities designating children in hospital for more than three months as either a predetermined group or individuals who might be in need of services.

Although, in line with arm (c) of Section 17, disabled children were generally seen as a priority group for services, the research team were concerned about the high priority given to children in arm (b) who might be at risk of significant harm alongside the exclusion of children under arm (a) whose development might be impaired, although this is clearly illegal in terms of the Act.

There was confusion about the status of disabled children as a separate group. Some authorities were unclear as to whether disability in its own right constituted eligibility for high priority services or whether disabled children had also to qualify under either arm (a) or (b).

There was a misinterpretation about the definition of 'statutory responsibilities' under Section 17, with most of our interviewees reserving this term for child protection cases or children looked after and seeing a two tier system of priority for service provision where what might have been traditionally termed 'preventive' work was seen as optional. It was also clear that a higher priority was given to children for whom the local authority already had some responsibility, such as those accommodated or in care. The contrast between the high frequency of priority grouping for children who had already committed offences as opposed to the low frequency of priority for those who might be at risk of offending, for example, was quite marked, suggesting that there was need for a more balanced relationship between significant harm and promotion of welfare. Such a view is supported by the substantial and cumulative research evidence about the multiple psycho-social problems which characterise the backgrounds of children entering the care system (see ***Department of Health (1991a) Patterns and Outcomes in Child Placement, HMSO).***

The interviews with senior managers confirmed that local authorities were struggling with how to implement the developmental links between the three arms of Section 17. Most felt that, although family support services were desirable to lower the threshold of significant harm, resource constraints precluded offering these services to any other than those already defined as being 'high risk' cases. This finding is also confirmed by a parallel study being undertaken for the Department of Health by Aldgate, Bradley and Hawley on the use of short term accommodation to help prevent family breakdown.

Providing services

The Children Act requires local authorities to facilitate the provision of services by others, including voluntary agencies, as well as by social services. The research explored two areas: the breadth of services on offer and origin of the providers.

Most of the local authorities said that they were providing a broad range of services, although it was outside the scope of the study to identify the quantity or quality of each facility offered. Providing family centres might mean one centre for 20 children in one authority or 20 for 500 children in another. The interviews confirmed that the picture was varied and also that services, though broad in scope, were often targeted on those children assessed as being at risk of significant harm. A minority had managed to offer services to a wider group. One authority had upgraded services for disabled children, confined team social work activity to significant harm investigations, and had asked voluntary agencies to organise open door centre-based services for different age groups of children.

There is therefore a complex picture emerging but it may be possible to detect a shift nationally towards a mixed economy of service provision. Tunstill and Ozolins provide a similar picture from the viewpoint of the voluntary sector (Tunstill and Ozolins 1994). The evidence from the study reported here suggests that social services are retaining control of services such as the provision of accommodation and investigative work but are developing partnerships with, for example, education and leisure in relation to after school provision and community-based youth activities and with the voluntaries in relation to centre-based provision such as family centres.

Implications for policy and service provision

1. The study suggests that there is further work to be done in helping local authorities in general, and social services in particular, to understand the potential of the inter-relationship between the three arms of need in Section 17.

2. The study revealed that some local authorities are narrowly defining 'in need' priority groups for services as children at risk of significant harm. Social services should be encouraged to review their policies and seek a wider definition.

3. More guidance needs to be given on the essential relationship between protection and family support: support services are **necessary** not optional if the aims of the Act are to be fully implemented.

4 The significance and consequences for service priority for disabled children as a category in their own right in Section 17 warrants more explanation. There is confusion about the circumstances under which disabled children might be a priority for services.

5 Social services have made real strides forward in working collaboratively with other departments of the local authority and with other professional bodies and are beginning to collaborate and consult voluntary agencies and user groups. This continuation of these partnerships should be encouraged and widened to include consultation with users.

6 There is a real problem about the accuracy of data available both to ascertain the extent of need and thereby make decisions for service provision and about the reliability of monitoring systems. This problem needs to be addressed urgently if Section 17 is to consolidate a need led service provision.

7 The principle of social services delivering services in collaboration with others also seems to be working well in some areas. The most efficient service delivery offering choice to the users seems to be where social services retain the overall control of planning but not necessarily of provision. There is evidence from this study and others (for example, ***Gibbons (1992) The Children act 1989 and Family Support, HMSO)*** of imaginative partnerships between social services and different agencies or organisations for service provision, especially for children with disabilities and for the under fives. The continuation of these developments should be actively encouraged.

8 Attention now needs to be paid to service provision in connection with new responsibilities such as children in hospital over 3 months.

The way forward

Since the completion of this study, there have been several significant developments in the evolution of family support services. The Audit Commission has produced an important report *Seen But Not Heard, Co-ordinating Child Health and Social Services for Children in Need,* (HMSO 1994) reiterating the value of working across the organisational divide in the provision of family support services. Tunstill and Ozolins have added to existing knowledge of the workings of a mixed economy approach through their study of the impact of the Children Act 1989 on the role of the voluntary organisations (see Tunstill and Ozolins 1994). This led to the establishment of The Family Support Network based at the Universities of Keele and East Anglia to provide research based information on services to statutory and voluntary agencies. The Social Services Inspectorate has undertaken a series of inspections in local authorities of the working of Section 17 of the Children Act 1989. Lastly, the Department of Health has now published the results of a series of important research studies on child protection (see Department of Health – *Protecting Children - Messages from Research,* HMSO, 1995). There are clear indications emerging from the findings of this research about the importance of underpinning child protection investigation with family support services. The research studies have 'questioned whether the balance between child protection and the range of supports and interventions available to professionals is correct.' (p.54). The Department of Health suggest that ' a more useful perspective' would mean that 'early work is viewed as an enquiry to establish whether the child in need might benefit from services. In only a proportion of cases will the child protection processes be called into play - the outcome of which will be family support or, in a minority of situations, child welfare for those living away from home. (p.54). Additionally, research on the use of short term accommodation for the Department of Health suggests that short term accommodation can facilitate and enhance family's management of their lives (see Bradley M. & Aldgate. ' Short term family based care for children in need' *Adoption and Fostering,* 18, 4, 24-29.)

It is likely that the central, though by no means unknown, challenge for childcare policy makers and practitioners in the next decade will be to rebalance the existing relationship between child protection and family support. It must be hoped that the increasing scope of research studies will enable researchers and practitioners to work together so that family support will be accorded its rightful place as the foundation stone of a just and effective child care system.

Appendix 1

Methodology

THE PURPOSE of the study was to provide a broad national picture of the range of approaches to implementation of Section 17 of the Children Act 1989 adopted by social services departments. The intention was to provide base line data from social services departments about a wide range of issues, including:

- How do authorities ascertain the extent of need?
- How are priorities for service determined?
- To what extent have local authorities developed a corporate strategy for services?
- Which services are available, what plans exist for developing services?

The conceptual framework for this study was set out in Chapter 1. There it was suggested that Section 17 represents a three-dimensional change in concept from earlier legislation:–

- from social work advice and counselling to a wider remit of service delivery;
- from prevention of reception into care to family support and promotion of welfare;
- from an undifferentiated group of children to a specific group of children in need.

The strategy was to examine how widely these three questions were defined by the local authorities in the study sample, i.e. to compare the individual authorities' stated definitions of children in need, which could be deemed 'normative' definitions of need and thereby to examine how those norms defined in one geographical area compare with those defined in another, thus including the wider concept of 'comparative need' (See Bradshaw 1972, Smith 1980).

Such broad questions required an equally broad and flexible approach in research design. It was therefore decided to use a combination of postal questionnaire, analysis of policy documents from social services and face to face interviews with senior and middle management staff. The combination of those three elements offered the most efficient method of gaining an overall picture of responses to implementation.

As this study began after October 1991, it was not possible to compare the strategies of social services departments in respect of their work with children and families before and after implementation of the Children Act. In some ways, such a before/after design offers only a simplistic solution to the problems of measuring changes to policy and service developments. The current study illustrated that local authority implementation work did not simply come 'on stream' immediately, and the study was able to engage in the changes in local authority responses over time, in particular, looking at the crossovers between the Children Act and Community Care Act.

Another possible method might have involved case studies of a smaller number of authorities. This approach was adopted in the recent study of four authorities by Giller (1993). In the current study it would have provided more detailed information, gained a wider range of personnel. However, such a design would not have yielded the breadth of information essential at this early stage of implementation. A study which focused on the analysis of documents alone for example Robbins (1990); would not have the advantages of including the responses of staff to such documents. Whilst such a study may have been more detailed, this would have been a at cost to external validity.

A combined approach

In practice, a combined approach was adopted.

1 The postal questionnaire ensured a national picture, and served as a counterbalance to any likely effects of over reporting from a small sample, one difficulty found in face to face interviews involving the recall of events (see Menneer, 1979). Additionally, any recall effects are at a minimum as this research focuses on a specific event, the implementation of the Children Act. Though it is right to recognise that this event was unique and outstanding in its own right, it has to be seen in the context of parallel major events equally influential on the work of social services. Planning by local authorities for the implementation of the Community Care Act was therefore a factor to be accounted for in the postal questionnaire.

2 The collection of policy documents provided a reference point for both questionnaire and interview. The documents provided a useful starting point from which to look at regional comparisons of the implementation of children in need.

3 The interview, administered at a point where it could take account of the postal data gave the opportunity to probe and check out written responses in order to optimise validity of all the research instruments. In addition, the strategy of including as large a sample as possible in the questionnaire and

a one in eight sampling frame for the interview was, in the view of the research team, likely to provide an accurate picture of practice surrounding Section 17.

The interview was semi-structured, which allowed for flexibility, and was more suited to the complex material within the study (see Fielding 1993). The research team took account of the issues of interviewer effects on the data collection process (see, for example, Hyman 1975). It was decided in line with the view of Denzin (1970) that there should be a combination of qualitative interviewing with other approaches to avoid bias.

It was also accepted by the research team that the collection of data in the form of accounts of activities or events rather than observation of direct behaviour means that problems of interpretation can exist, for example, that of low status respondents being 'researched' by higher status interviewers, where the effects of such 'asymmetric power relationships' can distort the data. The interviews in this study involved high status respondents, giving accounts of a high interest subject, a situation which maximises the reliability of data, see Mishler (1986).

Procedures for organising the study

The study had two stages:

1. The initial stage of the project, was based on a postal questionnaire to all 108 local authorities in England. These questionnaires were sent out in Autumn 1992. Authorities were also asked to send published policy documents relating to their definition of **children in need.**

2. Over the summer of 1993, the study followed up the postal questionnaire with face-to-face interviews with senior managers and team leaders from ten authorities.

Postal Questionnaire

This questionnaire was extensively developed in close collaboration with the Department of Health and was piloted with three authorities. The format was designed to incorporate some of the research instruments which had been used in the London Social Services Inspectorate's study carried out in 1991 (see SSI 1992). Its format also mirrored the Department of Health's own information-seeking exercise on the first year of implementation of other parts of the Act. The questionnaire carefully asked questions which were linked very closely to the intention and letter of the law. There was an in built expectation that authorities would be striving to fulfil their statutory duties in relation to implementing Section 17, since they had no choice but to comply with the law. The questionnaire was primarily designed to explore how far their planning and implementation had been developed, so that problems experienced could be identified to aid policy makers identify where further guidance might be needed. Given the complexity of the concept of children in need and the major change involved in moving from prevention to family support outlined in Chapter 1, our hypothesis was that it was extremely unlikely that implementation would be smooth or uniform across the country. Indeed the piloting confirmed that this supposition was indeed likely to be accurate.

A constraint of this approach designed to test the application of the law in practice was that the questionnaire was inevitably very complex and hardly user-friendly. Additionally, a minority of authorities told us that they were not even attempting to apply the law to change practice as intended in the spirit of the Act, but were approaching the task of ascertaining need in their area by seeing how far they could keep their pre-Children Act practice and adapt it to meet the minimum legal requirements. Such an approach almost flouted the intention of the Act but was a salutary lesson for the research design which was not open-ended but had assumed that the spirit and the letter of the law in relation to ascertaining need would have been obeyed. However, when data on the 82 authorities had been analysed, it was clear that this was a minority view confined to a handful of authorities. It was therefore possible to clarify with these authorities by telephone what their approach had been and to record their replies appropriately as missing data.

The questionnaire was divided into five sections, covering the following areas:

1 Ascertaining the extent of need in the Local Authority Area.

2 Use of data collection and consultation to formulate policy on **children in need.**

3 Establish high priorities for service provision.

4 Present future services for **children in need**.

5 The organisation of short term accommodation as a general service and for children with disabilities.

Although the questionnaire was lengthy, the sections could be separated, enabling more than one person to complete them. A substantial proportion of the questionnaire could be completed by simply ticking a list of alternatives. Respondents were also asked to enclose policy documents relating to children in need, plus any written material outlining social services referral categories for individual children.

The questionnaire included a reply slip to be returned on receipt, giving the research team an immediate contact point for follow up. Reminder letters were sent out after six weeks and telephone calls proved effective in encouraging late-returnees.

A high proportion of the questions were pre-coded. All coding and data entry was done by the research team using the SPSS-PC data analysis package, with help from the Oxford University Computing Centre.

(A copy of the questionnaire is available from the research team).

Interviews

The second phase of the study, which was developed from the replies in phase 1 was to administer semi-structured interviews to social services department staff from ten local authorities. It was thought important to see both senior managers at principal officer level as well as team leaders who would be directly implementing service provision and delivery.

Choosing which social services departments to interview was difficult because of their diversity on many fronts. The decision was made on a purposive basis to ensure representation in several key area. These were:

(a) demographic differences: e.g. to include representation from counties, cities and from different regions.

(b) organisational differences: e.g.. centrally controlled as opposed to devolved power and finances.

(c) differences in the pace of implementation of Section 17: three of the ten were well-advanced in their implementation, four had begun but were less advanced; and three were struggling to even begin to implement Section 17.

The judgements about these factors were made by the research team based on researcher ratings of different factors studied in the postal questionnaire.

The interviews were usually conducted by at least two of the research team, either at the social services department premises or in the University, with the exception of one authority where it proved impossible to meet face to face within the deadline so that telephone interviews were conducted instead. Interviews lasted on average one and a half to two hours. The first interview was held in May 1993, and the final interview took place in September 1993.

The interview schedule was divided into seven sections, covering a range of points:

1 Early arrangements and responses to Children Act implementation.

2 Data collection and Research Strategies in the Authority.

3 Consultation processes: within social services, within the local authority, with other organisations, with existing clients and with the wider community.

4 Organisational factors: how the type of organisational arrangements for service delivery might affect the style of service provision. Which groups of workers were involved in providing services for children in need? Details about the type of provision, for example, open access, or via individual referrals.

5 Prioritisation and categorisation of children in need: an area strongly identified as likely to show a diversity of approaches.

6 The development of the Children Act policy and planning.

7 Whether the idea of a mixed economy of care was incorporated into service delivery.

Some methodological issues related to responses

Questionnaire

The overall response rate to the self completion questionnaire was 80% (82/108), a good response rate to a postal questionnaire of this type when one considers the other research demands on social services departments at the time, and the length of the questionnaire.

There was a higher response rate from Southern as opposed to Northern authorities. This may have provided a bias in assessing the pace of the implementation process. It may well be that London and the South East had greater opportunities for wider consultation with policy makers than exist in other parts of England, and are in closer proximity to each other and to London based conferences.

One possible problem in relation to the data was the fact that a wide range of social services personnel had been given the responsibility for completing the questionnaire. These ranged from Assistant Directors, Policy Development Officers, Research Officers and Resource Managers. Although all could be classed as senior managers, their different operational remits might have resulted in differences in perspective, emphasis, and knowledge. It must also be recognised that in some cases, it would have been difficult for one person to provide a reply which would fully have represented an authority as a whole. The analysis of policy documents was, therefore, invaluable in providing an additional source of reliability to counter the effects of respondent variability. Additionally, it may well be that potentially difficult questions about implementation of Section 17 were more reliably dealt with in a postal questionnaire, as this might well have enabled managers to be more open about problematic areas in the implementation process, Overall, therefore, the responses to the postal questionnaire in relation to policy issues can be interpreted as a broad indication of local authorities position.

The sample represented the majority of authorities in England which adds reliability to the responses, although there is no way of knowing whether the authorities who did not complete the questionnaire would have different priorities concerning Children Act implementation from those who did take part in this study.

Interviews

The interviews were designed to highlight detailed information about individual implementation strategies.

The face to face interviews were conducted with a variety of personnel within 10 of the sample of social services departments. By accident rather than by design, all the senior managers interviewed were at Principal Officer level so there was less variability in role than in the postal questionnaire. There was also a fair degree of comparability of role in the middle managers although, as anticipated in the selection of authorities, differences in organisational structures did affect their remits.

As previously described, there was an intentional overlap between the interview and the postal questionnaire, so that consistency of response could be assessed. This proved operationally to be less straightforward since there was a time-lag between phases 1 and 2 and therefore respondents were talking about early implementation retrospectively. However, the time lag did give unforeseen opportunities to assess the evolving nature of the implementation process. As Chapter 2 showed, work on implementation was at a variety of levels, within and between a number of agencies so, by definition, no 'absolute' account would ever be possible or desirable. The interviews allowed respondents to reflect on the overall experience of being involved in a major shift in practice, from the initial establishment of 'implementation groups' to the acceptance of authority wide policy statements. They also allowed respondents to talk about future plans.

There remains the question of external validity, concerning the extent to which it is possible to generalise about the interview data. Given the range of factors taken into account in choosing the authorities, and given the telephone conversations with approximately twenty individuals regarding queries about the return of the questionnaire during the first phase, the research team were reasonably confident that the interview respondents represented an adequate diversity of authorities. Whether they were representative of a majority view of the 82 authorities is difficult to say' within such a small interview sample; it may in any case be the wrong question to ask, given the autonomy and diversity of social services nationally; rather they illustrated a range of approaches some authorities had taken in implementing Section 17.

An interim report on the findings of phase 1 was submitted to the Department of Health in November 1992. These early findings were included in Chapter 3 of ***Children Act 1989, A Report by the Secretaries of State for Health and for Wales on the Children Act 1989 in pursuance of their duties under Section 83(6) of the Act (1992) Cm 2144 HMSO 1992.***

Summary

The method used a combination of quantitative and qualitative information.

The postal questionnaire was designed to collect specific information from as wide a range of authorities as possible. This was backed up by documentary sources, so the main information elicited about the definition of **in need** was relatively unambiguous.

The detailed information on local authority strategy was gained by means of semi-structured interview, with a range of senior and middle managers. There was some overlap between questionnaire and interview schedule, to maximise reliability of the information. The interviews enabled the research team to explore the dynamic nature of implementation.

Appendix II

Table 1

How Local Authorities ascertained the total population of children in need. (n=82)

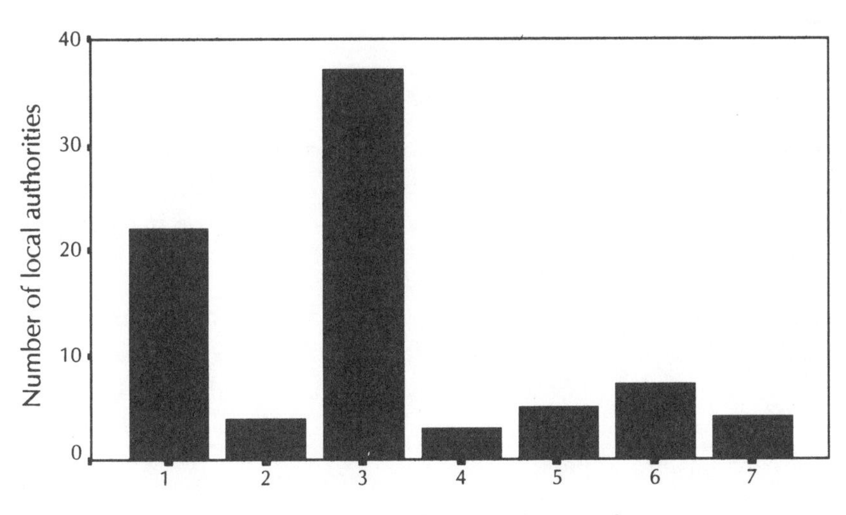

Key to Table

1	By referrals only.
2	By membership of pre-determined group.
3	By referrals *and* by membership of predetermined group.
4	By other means (e.g. using pre Children Act classifications).
5	By referrals *and* by membership of pre-determined groups *and* other means.
6	By referrals *and* other means.
7	No reply.

Table 2

Numbers of local authorities using predetermined groups of children for whom social services already have some responsibility to ascertain the extent of need in their area. (n=82)

Predetermined group	No of LA's (of 82)	Percentage (of 82 LA's)
Children at risk of significant harm	62	76
Children at risk of neglect	61	74
Children in care	60	73
Children accommodated under s.20	59	72
Young people on remand	57	70
Children/young people once in care	55	67
Children in hospital over 3 months	33	40
Privately fostered children	31	38

Note

Predetermined groups are **not** mutually exclusive, so that there is the possibility of 100% response rate for each predetermined group.

Table 3

Numbers of local authorities using predetermined group of children in the community to ascertain the extent of need in their area. (n=82)

Predetermined group	No of LA's (of 82)	Percentage of LA's (of 82)
Children with disabilities	56	68
Children with special educational needs	45	55
Children with special health needs	40	49
Young people at risk of criminal acts	40	49
Young people in penal system	36	44
Children with difficult family relationships	33	40
Children at risk/has HIV/Aids	33	40
Carers with disabilities	32	39
Homeless families	29	35
Drug/solvent abusing children	27	33
Families in bed and breakfast accommodation	24	29
Children excluded from school	24	29
Carers with mental illness	23	28
Children in low income families	22	27
Children in substandard housing	22	27
Young people in bed and breakfast accommodation	21	26
Children under 8	17	21
Black/ethnic minority children	17	21
School truants	16	19
One parent families	15	18
Children in specific geographical areas	13	16
Unemployed parents	12	15
Families with utilities cut off	12	15
Children with divorcing parents	10	12
Adopted children	10	12
Children of Travellers	9	11
Children with English as second language	7	9
Children in independent school	6	7

Note

Predetermined groups are **not** mutually exclusive, so that there is the possibility of 100% response rate for each predetermined group.

Table 4

Mean number of agencies consulted by social services, by region. (n=82)

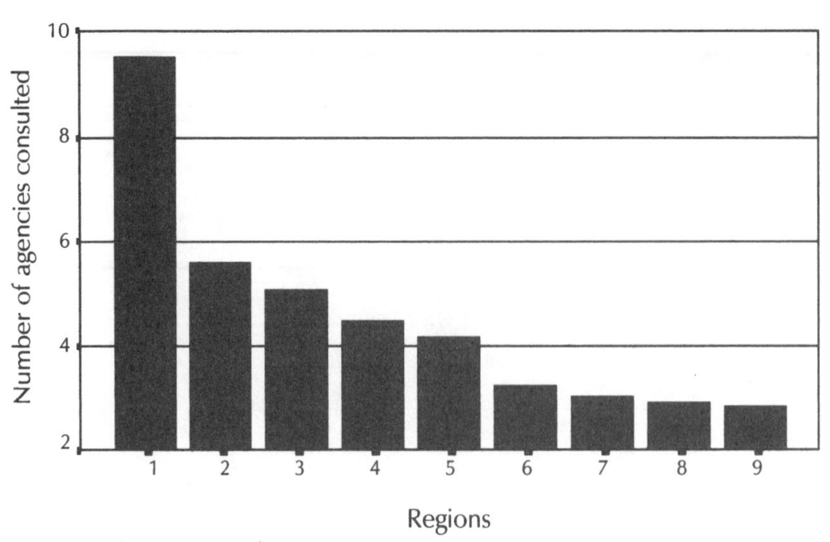

Key to Regions

1	South West.
2	London.
3	Yorks/Humberside.
4	West Midlands.
5	Southern.
6	Northern.
7	North West
8	East Midlands
9	Thames/Anglia

Table 5

Numbers of social services departments holding consultation meetings with other local authority departments or outside agencies. (n=82)

Department or agency consulted	Number of LA's (of 82)	Percentage of LA's (of 82)
Education	74	90
Health	70	85
Housing	60	73
Leisure and recreation	48	58
Probation	41	50
Police	40	49
Voluntary agencies	37	45
Within SSD	36	44
Other	21	26
Social security	13	16
Plannings	12	15
Did not consult	12	15
Transport	4	5
Employment	4	5
Other statutory agency	4	5

Note

Agencies or departments are **not** mutually exclusive, so that there is the possibility of 100% response rate for each department or agency consulted.

Table 6

Numbers of local authority departments or outside agencies consulted by social services departments. (n=82)

Number of departments or agencies consulted	Number of SSD's	Percentage of SSD's
No agency consulted	12	15
1 agency consulted	6	7
2-3 agencies consulted	10	12
4-6 agencies consulted	38	46
7 and over agencies consulted	16	20
Total	**82**	**100%**

Table 7
Social services and other departments who have agreed common criteria for registration of disabled children. (n=82)

Local authority departments who have agreed common criteria	Number of SSD's (of 82)	Percentage of SSD's (of 82)
No registration agreed yet	27	33
SSD + health and education and voluntary sector	24	29
SSD + health and education	17	21
SSD + health and education, voluntary sector and/or others	6	7
SSD + health	3	4
Missing data	5	6
Total	**82**	**100%**

Table 8
Numbers of social services departments circulating documents to local authority departments or outside agencies. (n=82)

Department or agencies given documents	Number of SSD's (of 82)	Percentage of SSD's (of 82)
Education	65	79
Health	55	67
Housing	53	65
Social Services	46	56
Voluntaries	43	52
Leisure and Recreation	41	50
Probation	36	44
Police	33	40
Other LA department	16	20
Planning	13	16
Social Security	5	6
Employment	5	6
Other statutory	5	6
Transport	3	4

Note
Agencies or departments are **not** mutually exclusive, so that there is the possibility of 100% response rate for each agency or department given documents.

Table 9
Social Services' assessment of the consultation process with other local authority depatments or outside agencies. (n=82)

Department or agency consulted	Numbers and percentages of social services departments (of 82)							
	Excellent		**Acceptable**		**Unsatisfactory information**		**Don't know/ missing information**	
	Numbers of SSD's	% of SSD's	Numbers of SSD's	% of SSD's	Numbers of SSD's	% of SSD's	Numbers of SSD's	% of SSD's
Health	24	29	43	53	5	6	10	12
Education	16	20	51	62	5	6	10	12
Probation	14	17	27	33	1	1	40	49
Housing	13	16	40	49	11	13	18	22
Police	9	11	32	39	41	50	–	–
Leisure/recreation	8	10	33	40	11	13	30	37
Planning	3	4	16	19	3	4	60	73
Transport	2	2	10	12	1	1	69	85

Note
Departments/agencies are **not** mutually exclusive, so that there is the possibility of 100% response rate for each department or agency consulted.

Table 10

Characteristics of individual children which lead social services to accord children high priority for access to services. (n=82)

Characteristic	No of SSD's (of 82)	Percentage of SSD's (of 82)
Child at risk of abuse	63	77
Child at risk of neglect	63	77
Child with a disability	56	68
Child who has offended	49	60
Child who is HIV+	37	45
Child in low income family	35	43
Child with behaviour problems	34	41
Child, risk of offending	32	39
Child with developmental problems	30	37
Focus of problems is with the parents	29	35
Child who is abusing drugs	29	35
Child who is homeless	13	16
Parents have marital/relationship problems	7	9
Child lives in bad housing	5	6

Note

Characteristics are **not** mutually exclusive, so that there is the possibility of 100% response rate for each characteristic.

Table 11

High prioritised groups of children for whom social services already have some responsibility. (n=82)

	No of SSD's (of 82)	Percentage of SSD's (of 82)
Children at risk of significant harm	64	78
Children at risk of neglect	61	74
Children in care	61	74
Children accommodated under s.20	60	73
Children on remand	57	70
Childrenpreviously in care/accommodation	52	63
Children in hospital more than three months	25	30
Privately fostered children	23	28

Note

High priority groups are **not** mutually exclusive, so that there is the possibility of 100% response rate for each group.

Table 12

High prioritised groups of children in the community. (n=82)

Family stability issues	Number of SSD's (of 82)	Percentage of SSD's (of 82)
Children with behavioural problems	10	12
Parents with marital/relationship problems	8	10
Children with divorcing parents	5	6
Housing issues		
Homeless families	20	24
Children in bed and breakfast accommodtion	12	15
Children in substandard housing	10	12
Children living in homes with gas/electricity/water disconnected	10	12
Poverty issues		
Children in low income families	8	10
Children in one parent families	8	10
Children with unemployed parents	6	7
Disability/health issues		
Children with disabilities	44	54
Children with special health needs	23	28
Children with special educational needs	6	24
Education issues		
Children excluded from school	9	11
Children who truant	7	9
Children in independent schools	5	6
Ethnic/linguistic minorities		
Ethnic minority/black children	8	10
Children with English as second language	2	2
Involvement in crime issues		
At risk of involvement in crime	27	33
Young people in penal system	27	33
Other children		
Children at risk of HIV/AIDS	25	30
Children under 8	13	16
Refugee children	9	11
Children in specific geographic areas	6	7

Note

High priority groups are **not** mutually exclusive, so that there is the possibility of 100% response rate for each group.

Table 13

Categories of individual referrals of children who have received a high priority for service provision. (n=82)

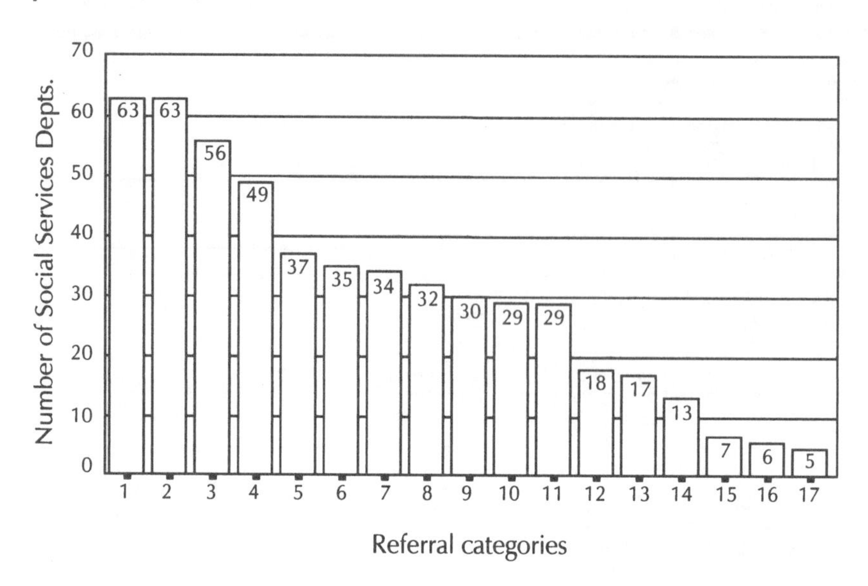

Key to referral categories

1	Child at risk of neglect.
2	Child at risk of abuse.
3	Child with a disability.
4	Child who has offended.
5	Child who is HIV+.
6	Child in low income family.
7	Child with behaviour problems.
8	Child at risk of offending.
9	Child with development problem.
10	Child who is abusing drugs.
11	Focus of the problem is with the parent/s.
12	Child with educational problems.
13	Child with general health problems.
14	Child who is homeless.
15	Parents have marital/relationship problems.
16	Child lives in specified geographical area.
17	Child lives in poor housing.

Table 14
Numbers of Local Authorities providing the following services. (n=82)

Service	No of LA's	Percentage of LA's
Respite care, disabled children	80	98
Full time accommodation for children looked after	80	98
Foster care for child looked after	80	98
Section 17 payments	80	98
Child protection services	79	96
Advice & guidance to disabled child and parents	77	94
Advice & guidance to parents (general)	76	93
Advice/assistance, young person ceasing to be looked after	76	93
Advice & guidance to children & young people (in general)	75	91
Domiciliary care	74	90
Advice & guidance to disabled/ill parents	74	90
Respite care for children (general)	72	88
Sponsored childminding	71	87
Supervised activities	71	87
Help wih travel where needed	70	85
Full tme accommodation, disabled children	69	84
Accommodation, young person ceasing to be looked after	68	83
Child psychiatric/guidance	67	82
Family centres	66	80
Home visiting	64	78
Preparing disabled children for independence	64	78
Day nurseries	61	74
Family aides	61	74
Supervision for matrimonial cases	55	67
Holiday actvities	55	67
Help child and family have holidays	51	62
Education for child looked after, not at school	45	55
Befriending	44	54
Laundry services	41	50
Out of school care	39	48

Note
Services are **not** mutually exclusive, so that there is the possibility of 100% response rate for each service.

Table 15
Range of services used by social services showing who provides these.

	Provided by SSD	Provided by other LA Dept	Services sub-contracted to voluntary agency	Services sub-contracted to private company	Ad hoc purchase of service/ places from other organisations as requested	Other
Day nurseries	57	22	13	7	34	–
Family centres	62	4	39	–	8	1
Home visiting	66	9	29	–	1	2
Befriending	31	3	28	–	7	1
Family aides	64	1	2	2	–	–
Domiciliary care	78	1	5	1	7	1
Laundry services	34	2	–	–	4	2
Sponsored childminding	63	6	4	–	11	1
Child protection services	81	13	22	–	4	4
Advice/guidance counselling to parents – general	81	18	29	–	4	4
Advice/counselling to children with disabilities and parents	79	29	31	–	5	5
Preparing children with disabilities for independence (eg leaving school, going to sheltered accommodation)	75	37	14	–	8	2
Child psychiatry/guidance	43	36	2	—	11	15
Supervision for matrimonial cases	57	8	2	–	–	6
Short term accommodation (respite care) for children (general)	76	6	11	1	24	–
Short term accommodation (respite care) for children with disabilities	79	7	30	4	30	2

Table 15 – *continued*
Range of services used by social services showing who provides these.

	Provided by SSD	Provided by other LA Dept	Services sub-contracted to voluntary agency	Services sub-contracted to private company	Ad hoc purchase of service/ places from other organisa-tions as requested	Other
Full time accommodation for children looked after (general)	80	7	22	10	48	–
Full time accommodation for children with disabilities	66	13	22	8	43	–
Foster care for children looked after	81	3	10	1	25	–
Accommodation for young people ceasing to be looked after	48	39	32	1	29	1
Advice and assistance for young people ceasing to be looked after	79	13	27	1	5	–
Education for children 'looked after' who are not attending day school	27	56	2	–	4	–
Holiday activities	39	47	28	3	27	1
Supervised activities (eg IT groups)	69	13	15	–	11	3
Help with travel/transport where needed	70	14	4	3	6	–
Help to enable child and family to have a holiday	51	–	5	–	14	–
Financial payments under Section 17	81	1	1	–	–	–
Details of any other services (specify)	4	–	1	–	–	1

Table 16
Modes of provision of family centres by local authorities. (n=82)

(Frequencies and percentages shown)

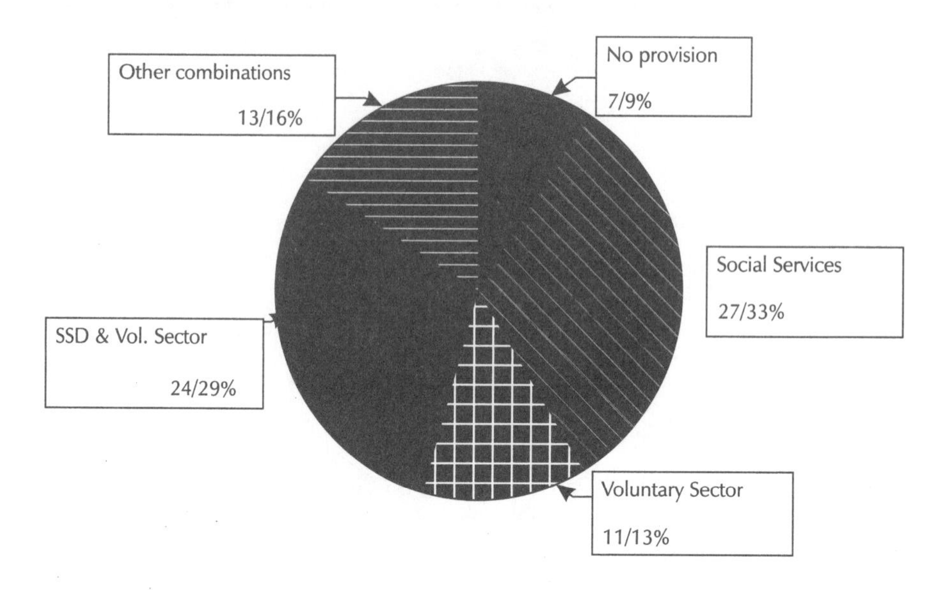

Table 17
Modes of provision of out of school care by local authorities. (n=82)

(Frequencies and percentages shown)

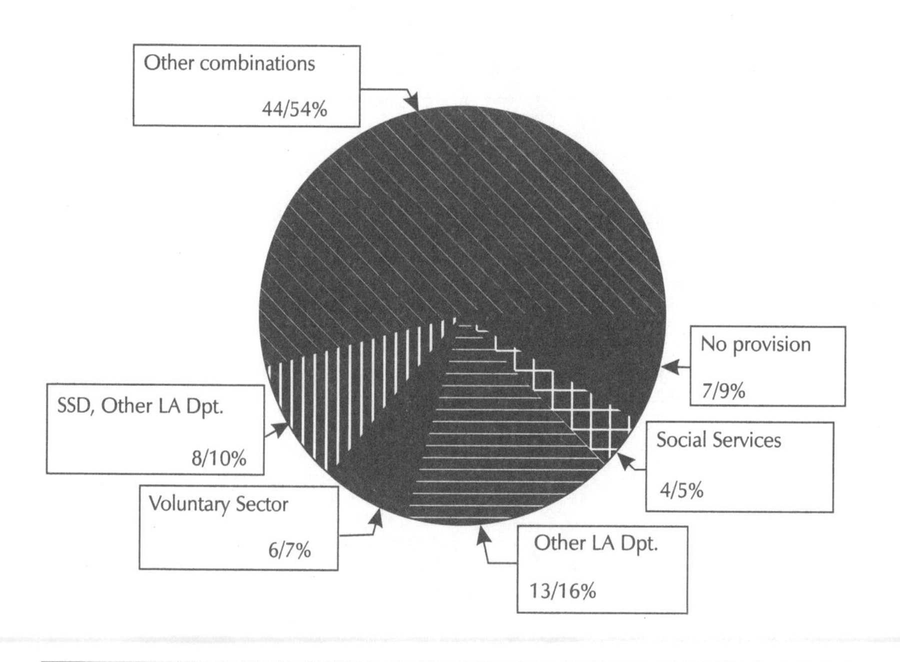

Table 18

Modes of provision of respite care for children with disabilities by local authorities. (n=82)

(Frequencies and percentages shown)

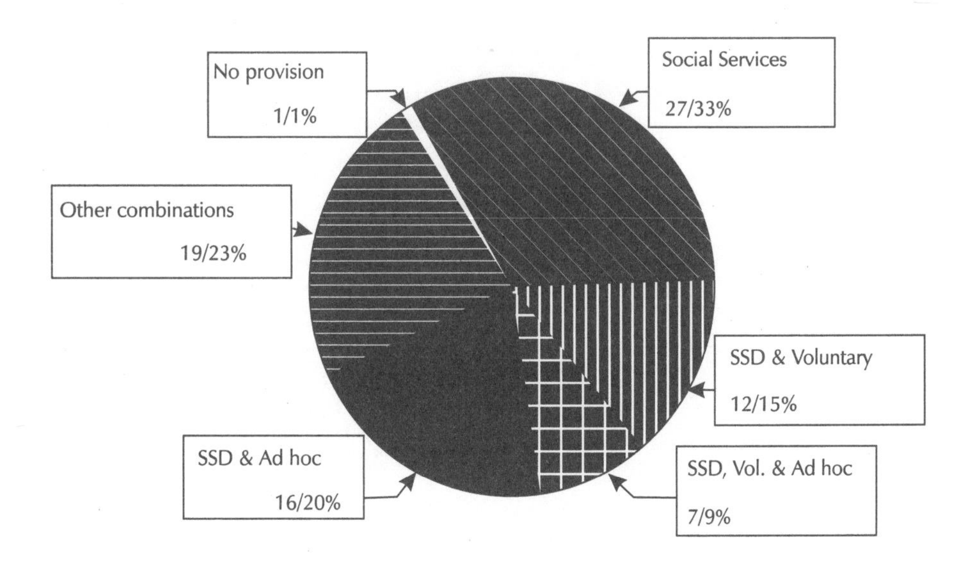

Table 19

Modes of provision of general respite care by local authorities. (n=82)

(Frequencies and percentages shown)

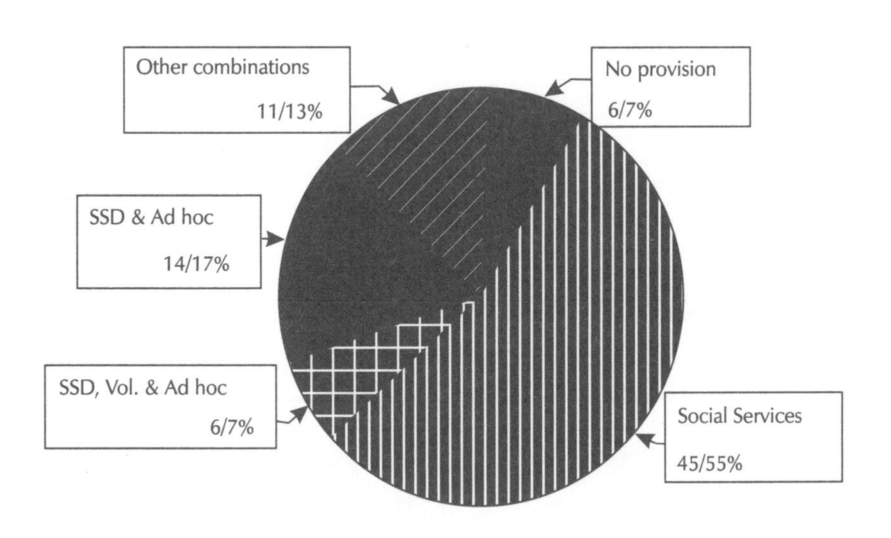

Bibliography

Aldgate, J. (1993), 'Respite care for children – an old remedy in a new package', in Marsh, P. and Triseliotis, J. (eds), *Prevention and Reunification in Child Care,* London, Batsford.

Aldgate, J. and Heath, A. F. (1992), *The Educational Progress of Children in Foster Care*, Final Report to the ESRC.

Audit Commission, (1994), *Seen but Not Heard – Co-ordinating Community Child Health and Social Services for Children in Need,* London, HMSO.

Bebbington, A. and Miles, J. (1989), 'The background of children who enter local authority care', *British Journal of Social Work*, 19, 5, pp. 349-368.

Billis, D. (1984), *Welfare Bureaucracies*, London, Heinemann.

Bradley, M. and Aldgate, J. (1994), 'Short term family based care for children in need', *Adoption and Fostering*, 18, 4, pp. 24-29.

Bradshaw, J. (1972), 'The concept of social need', in Fitzgerald, M. et al. *Welfare in Action*, London, Routledge and Kegan Paul, in association with the Open University Press, Milton Keynes.

Bradshaw, J. (1990), *Child Poverty and Deprivation in The UK*, London, National Children's Bureau.

Cannan, C. (1993), *Changing Families, Changing Welfare Family Centres and The Welfare State*, Brighton, Harvester Wheatsheaf.

Cm 2144 (1992), *Children Act 1989, A Report by the Secretaries of State for Health for England and for Wales, on the Childen Act 1989 in Pursuance of Their Duties under Section 83(6) of the Act*, London, HMSO.

Cm 3703 (1968), Seebohm, F. (Chair), *Report of the Committee on Local Authority and Allied Services*, London, HMSO.

Cox, A., Pound, A. and Puckering, C. (1991), 'Newpin: A befriending scheme and therapeutic network for carers of young children' in Gibbons, J. (ed), *The Children Act and Family Support: Principles into Practice*, London, HMSO.

Department of Health and Social Security (1985), *Social Work Decisions in Child Care, Recent Research Findings and their Implications*, London, HMSO.

Department of Health (1989), *The Care of Children: Principles and Practice in Regulations and Guidance*, London, HMSO.

Department of Health (1991a), *Patterns and Outcomes in Child Placement: Messages From Current Research and their Implications*, London, HMSO.

Department of Health (1991b), *The Children Act 1989, Guidance and Regulations, Volume 2, Family Support, Day Care and Educational Provision for Young Children*, London, HMSO.

Department of Health (1991c), *Working Together under the Children Act 1989, A Guide to Arrangements for Inter-Agency Co-operation for the Protection of Children from Abuse*, London, HMSO.

Department of Health (1991d), *The Children Act 1989, Guidance and Regulations, Volume 6, Children with Disabilities*, London, HMSO.

Department of Health (1995), *Protecting Chidren – Messages from Research*, London, HMSO.

Denzin, N. (1993), *The Research Act*, Chicago, McGraw-Hill.

Family and Child Care Law Training Group (1989), *Training Together: A Training Curriculum for the Children Act 1989*, London, LBTC/LBCRPC, 11/89.

Fielding, N. (1993), 'Qualitative interviewing', in Gilbert, N. (ed), *Researching Social Life*, London, Sage.

Farmer, E. and Parker, R. (1991), *Trials and Tribulations*, London, HMSO.

Fox Harding, L. (1991), *Perspectives in Child Care Policy*, London, Longman.

Fuller, R. (1987), *Research in Prevention: A Research Note*, Stirling University, Social Work Research Centre.

Fuller, R. (1989), 'Problems and possibilities in studying preventive work', *Adoption and Fostering*, 13, 1, pp. 9-13.

Fuller, R. (1992), *In Search of Prevention*, Aldershot, Avebury.

Gardner, R. (1992), *Preventing Family Breakdown*, London, National Children's Bureau.

George, V. and Wilding, P. (1985), *Ideology and Social Welfare*, (2nd Edition), London, Routledge and Kegan Paul.

Gibbons, J., et al. (1990), *Family Support and Prevention: Studies in Local Areas*, London, HMSO.

Gibbons, J. (1992), (ed), *The Children Act 1989 and Family Support – Principles into Practice*, London, HMSO.

Giller, H. (1993), *Children in Need, Definition, Management and Monitoring A Report for the Department of Health, Social Information Systems*, London, and the Department of Health.

Hallett, C. and Stevenson, O. (1980), *Child Abuse: Aspects of Interprofessional Co-operation*, London, Allen and Unwin.

Hardiker, P., Exton, K. and Barker, M. (1991a), *Policies and Practice in Preventive Child Care*, Aldershot, Gower.

Hardiker, P., Exton, K. and Barker, M. (1991b), 'The social policy contexts of prevention in child care', *British Journal of Social Work*, 21, 4, pp. 341-359.

Heath, A. F., Colton, M.J. and Aldgate, J. (1989), 'The education of children in and out of care', *British Journal of Social Work*, 19, 1, pp. 447-640.

Heywood, J. (1965), *Children in Care*, London, Routledge Kegan Paul.

Holman, R. (1988), *Putting Families First: Prevention and Child Care, A Study of Prevention by Statutory and Voluntary Agencies*, Basingstoke Macmillan.

Hyman, H. (ed). (1975), *Interviewing in Social Research*, Chicago and London, University of Chicago Press.

Jones, M.A. (1976), *A Second Chance for Families: Five Years Later*, New York, Research Centre, Child Welfare League of America.

Jones, D., Sharland, E., Seal, H., Croucher, M. and Aldgate J. (1993), *Early Intervention in Child Sexual Abuse Cases*, Final Report to the Department of Health.

Jordan, B. (1987/88), 'Why is Prevention Neglected?', *Family Rights Group Bulletin*, London, Family Rights Group.

King, M. and Piper C. (1990), *How the Law Thinks about Children*, Aldershot, Gower.

Kumar, V. (1993), *Poverty and Inequality in the UK, The Effects on Children*, London, National Children's Bureau.

Macleod, V. (1982), *Whose Child? The Family in Child Care Legislation and Social Work Practice*, Occasional Paper 11, London, Study Commission on the Family.

McGowan, B. and Meezan, W. (1983), *Child Welfare: Current Dilemmas, Future Directions*, New York, F. E. Peacock, Inc.

Menneer, P. (1979), 'Retrospective Data in Survey Research' in Moss, L. and Goldstein, H. (eds), *The Recall Method in Social Surveys*, London, University of London Institute of Education.

Mishler, E. (1986), *Research Interviewing*, Cambridge, Massachusetts and London, Harvard Univesity Press.

Orlik, C., Robinson, C., Russel, O. (1991), *A Survey of Family Based Respite Care Schemes in the UK*, Bristol University, Norah Fry Research Centre.

Packman, J. (1975), *The Child's Generation: Child Care Policy From Curtis to Houghton*, Oxford, Basil Blackwell.

Packman, J. (1986), *Who Needs Care? Social Work Decisions about Children*, Oxford, Basil Blackwell.

Packman, J. and Jordan, B. (1991), 'The Children Act: looking forward, looking back', *British Journal of Social Work*, 21, 2, pp. 315-327.

Parker, R.A. (ed.), (1980), *Caring for Separated Children*, Basingstoke, Macmillan.

Parker, R.,Ward, H., Jackson, S., Aldgate, J. and Wedge, P., (1991), (eds), *Looking After Children – Assessing Outcomes in Child Care*, London, HMSO.

Robbins, D. (1990), *Putting it in Writing: A Review of English Local Authorities' Child Care Policy Statements*, London, SS1, HMSO.

Rose, W. (1992) Foreword in Gibbons, op. cit.

Shaw, M., Masson, J. and Brocklesby, E., (1991), *Children in Need and Their Families: A New Approach, A Guide to Part III of the Children Act 1989 for Local Authority Councillors*, School of Social Work, University of Leicester.

Short, R. (chair) (1984), *Second Report from the Social Services Committee Session 1983-1984*, Children in Care, 360-II, London, HMSO.

Smith, G. (1980), *Social Need Policy, Practice and Research*, London, Routledge and Kegan Paul.

Smith, T. (1992), 'Family Centres, Children in Need and the Children Act 1982', in Gibbons, J. op. cit.

Social Services Inspectorate London Region (1992), *Capitalising on the Act, A Working Party Report on the Implementation of the Children Act 1989 in London*, London, HMSO.

Stalker, K. (1990), *Share the Care: An Evaluation of a Family Based Respite Care Scheme*, London, Jessica Kingsley.

Thoburn, J. (1980), *Captive Clients: Social Work with Families of Children Home on Trial*, London, Routledge Kegan Paul.

Tunstill, J. (1991), 'The Children Act and the voluntary child care sector', Children and Society, vol. 5 1 pp. 374-384.

Tunstill, J. (1992, 'Local authority policies on children in need' in Gibbons, J. (ed.), (1992), op. cit.

Tunstill, J. and Ozolins, R. (1994), *Voluntary Child Care Organisations after the 1989 Children Act*, Univesity of East Anglia/National Council of Voluntary Child Care Organisations.

Utting, D., et al. (1993), *Crime and the Family: Improving Child Rearing and Preventing Delinquency*, London, Family Policy Studies Centre.

Van der Eyken, W. (1984), *Day Nurseries in Action, a National Study of Local Authority Day Nurseries in England, 1975-1983*, Bristol University, Department of Health Research Unit.

Watson, S. (1973), 'The Children's Department and the 1963 Act in Stroud', in Watson, S. (1973), (ed), *Services for Children and Their Families: Aspects of Child Care for Social Workers*, Oxford, Pergamon Press.

Printed in the United Kingdom for TSO
N126620 C3 1/03 9385 18651